Mountains of Kenya

MOUNTAINS OF KENYA

PETER ROBSON

Published for the Mountain Club of Kenya

EAST AFRICAN PUBLISHING HOUSE

First published in 1969 for the Mountain Club of Kenya
by the East African Publishing House, P.O. Box 30571, Nairobi

Printed and made in Kenya by Kenya Litho Ltd
P.O. Box 775, Nairobi, Kenya

Foreword

By the Hon. Humphrey Slade, Speaker of the Kenya National Assembly and Patron of the Mountain Club of Kenya

By producing this book for the Mountain Club of Kenya, Peter Robson has rendered a great service.

Levavi oculos. The Psalmist knew the spiritual comfort, as well as the physical pleasure, that can be derived from walking on mountains; and many of us have known it too. It is something much more than the mere satisfaction of exercise and achievement. There is the awe-inspiring beauty, in fine weather or in foul, and the immensity which, like the vastness of the sea, cuts one down to size. Mountains talk to those who love them; and they speak words of comfort which are remembered long after they were spoken.

It is one thing, however, to have a passion for mountains, and another to know where to find them and how to reach them, especially for those who may not be staying long or who would like to go far afield. Hence the need of this book, which will not only inspire people to explore our mountains but will also provide them with the most valuable practical advice on how to do so.

The mountains and hills of Kenya are among the most beautiful features of a very beautiful country. There are so many which present, in Peter Robson's words, "a reasonable vertical difference between the summit and the level of the surrounding countryside". It is, in fact, characteristic of our mountains that they rise abruptly to great heights; and by so doing, they offer both grandeur and challenge. Moreover, because of this rapidly changing altitude, they contain within short distances fascinating variations of fauna and flora. A walker may travel through Africa horizontally for many miles without seeing much change or seeming to get anywhere; but travel as near vertically as he can, and he will see, from plains through forest to moorland and even glacier, such variety of creation within every mile as to take away any breath that he may have to spare.

Readers of this book who are already here will now find new and exciting adventures opened up to them, with the minima of discomfort and danger. Readers who have never yet visited Kenya will now be tempted to do so. And those of us whose legs are not as strong for hills as they were, will, as we read, yet feel that we stretch them again in high and wondrous places.

Preface

For a number of years the Mountain Club of Kenya has been anxious to supplement its rock climbing hand-books by a guide book to the 'mountains of Kenya designed primarily for the hill climber. This ambitious project owed its origin primarily to John Johnson. It was his enthusiasm which resulted in the initial collection of a great deal of information about routes from members of the Club and from informants in the administration and elsewhere. The outcome was a preliminary mimeographed guide book which appeared in 1966 and is now out of print. The reception given to that initial survey has stimulated the production of a completely revised and much expanded volume which it is hoped will be of interest not only to members of the Club, but also to the general public. The route descriptions are prefaced by a brief history of the European discovery and exploration of the East African mountains. The emphasis of this survey is on the mountains of Kenya, but the exploration of the higher mountains of Tanzania and Uganda is also briefly reviewed. An attempt has been made to establish the dates of the first recorded ascents by a search of the literature. In many cases it has also been possible to provide information on the meanings of the names of the mountains and on legends associated with them. The book includes a selected bibliography of some of the more interesting works which record exploration and travel among the mountains of East Africa.

To decide on which hills to include in a mountain guide book is, of course, difficult, but some selection must be made. One criterion might be the interest of the ascents, but this is hardly a principle on which there would be general agreement. Broadly speaking, the approach adopted in the preparation of this book has been to include all hills higher than 7000 ft. subject to there being a reasonable vertical difference between the summit and the level of the surrounding countryside. This procedure may have resulted in the exclusion of some hills which afford enjoyable walking expeditions; on the other hand, a few of the summits included may be of only limited interest to the mountain walker. On the basis of the criterion, a number of "tops" over 7000 ft. find no place, as in the Loita Highlands. However, some 7000 ft. summits are included which involve a vertical ascent of only a few hundred feet, usually because they afford a good view point. Where summits are forested, and there is no view, this has been indicated. A few slightly lower hills have also found a place in the guide where the hills in question are of particular interest and the vertical ascent is substantial. Nzaui, only 6000 ft., is one such hill. Although it is relatively low, it rises up from the south as a most spectacular peak, with big rock precipices. There are certainly a number of other lower hills which might on these grounds also have a claim to be included, like some of the south Teita hills near the main road inland from Mombasa, and others in the north east and on the Ethiopian border. However, a line has to be drawn somewhere. Apologies are extended to anyone whose favourite smaller hills have been excluded.

Although the book is concerned mainly with the mountains of Kenya, room has been found, on the ground of their popularity with Kenya climbers, for a few accounts of mountains which lie outside Kenya's borders. Most of these mountains can be reached in a long week-end from Nairobi, although a few, like Moroto and Kadam, require a longer period. Of course, not all of the Kenya mountains listed in this guide can be climbed in a long week-end from Nairobi. Those in the far north require far longer unless one uses a light aeroplane to reach nearby airstrips.

From the table of Contents it will be seen that the mountains are divided into ten major geographical groupings, apart from Mount Kenya. Within these groupings the mountains are numbered serially and they are described in that order in the text. The numbers are keyed to the map on page 74. The Index to the map, which will be found on page 75, can conveniently be used to locate the route descriptions for any of the mountains included in the guide.

In most cases times of ascent are given for the routes described. These time, presuppose a fit person, acclimatised to the altitude which is often considerable and not carrying heavy loads. *The references to the left or right bank of rivers refer to the "true" right or left bank.*

None of the routes included in the Guide requires rock climbing to reach the summit although in one or two cases, like the Kinangop, an airy scramble may be called for. Since some of the finest of Kenya's mountain walking excursions are to be found in the Mount Kenya area, the book includes information on access to the main peaks of this area, and indicates some of the more popular approaches and circuits. However, those who intend to undertake rock-climbing excursions on the central peaks of Mount Kenya or who require detailed information on their geology, glaciology, flora and fauna should consult the *Guide Book to Mount Kenya and Kilimanjaro* which is published by the Mountain Club of Kenya.

The preparation of the route descriptions in this guide book would not have been possible without the help of many persons. A large number of the routes are based on contributions from members of the Mountain Club and others who initially responded to John Johnson's requests for information. Subsequently Robert Chambers was instrumental in collecting much additional information, particularly for the more northerly mountains. In editing this material I received much help from fellow members of the Mountain Club of Kenya and from others. Much valuable help was provided by Patrick Ferguson in the initial compilation of the data. Particular thanks are due to John Loxton, Deputy Director of the Survey of Kenya and a member of the MCK. From the files of the Survey of Kenya he was able to provide many additional routes and he gave access to the field reports of some of the early map makers who were responsible for making some of the first recorded ascents. In addition he most generously undertook to have the Index Map drawn and he readily devoted much time to answering questions on topographical matters.

In writing the section on the exploration of the mountains, I have had much help from Mr. A. T. Matson, an authority on the exploration and the history of Kenya who was unsparing of his time and knowledge. Dr. Alan Jacobs, an authority on the Maasai, supplied the meanings of many of the Maasai place names and checked the meaning of others. Others who generously provided help on place names include: Mr. Ole Saibull, Mr. E. J. Anderson, Mr. C. J. Thomas, Mr. F. A. Gibbon, Mr. C. E. Barnett and Mr. H. A. Fosbrooke.

1. *Mountain Walking in Kenya*

Without doubt, the mountains of Kenya afford some of the finest hill and mountain expeditions to be found anywhere in the world. Of the ascents described in this book, none demands rock climbing; all are mountain walking expeditions. But although many of the ascents are certainly "an easy day for a lady", some are arduous by reason of terrain, length, altitude or heat. The following comments are offered primarily for those who are approaching the Kenya hills for the first time, perhaps without companions who are familiar with local conditions and the special features of climbing on the Equator.

From the route descriptions it will be seen that most of the mountains described in the guide book can be reached by an ordinary saloon car and virtually all by enterprising private cars (EPCs). But a few of the mountains can only be reached by very rough safaris for which a Land Rover or similar vehicle is essential. Most of these mountains lie in the far north. Many of the mountains are not far from trading centres through which, if necessary, mechanical or other assistance might be summoned. But it should be borne in mind that some of Kenya's mountains, particularly those of the northern frontier, are in remote, semi arid areas which are only sparsely inhabited by pastoral peoples. When visiting these areas it is prudent to take adequate reserves of water, petrol and spares, and if possible to travel with more than one car. In a few instances, for example to proceed north of Isiolo, the administration requires that parties should include at least two cars. A breakdown in these remote areas could involve a long and arduous walk-out for assistance. In the far north, rivers are often not bridged and sudden rain may necessitate a wait until the rivers have fallen.

When to go

Although Kenya weather is notoriously good, there are distinct seasonal changes which affect climbing. Over the western Kenya Highlands rain occurs mainly from March or April to September or October. Most of the highlands area east of the Aberdare range has two rainy seasons. Here the long rains fall from March or April until May. The not so well marked secondary rains, known as the short rains, occur from late October to mid December. In this eastern region there are also two different dry seasons. That cf June to September is cloudy and cool, while that of January to March is sunny and warm.

Travel on the highest mountains such as Kenya, the Aberdares and Elgon, should not be attempted during the rainy seasons when conditions may become distinctly unpleasant. However, many of the lesser mountains can be climbed throughout the year, for during the rains, rain is not uninterrupted. Generally the rain is in the form of showers or thunderstorms broken by several hours of sunshine. In the highlands the mornings are usually fine; the rain occurs mainly during the afternoons and evenings. Nevertheless, although climbing is certainly carried on during the rains, it is mainly undertaken during the dry period. This is not merely because the mountains may be sometimes uncomfortable during the rains but also because of difficulties of access. Many of the access roads are not all-weather and may become impassable, and some are closed to prevent damage during the rains. But many mountains which lie near the tarmac or on all-weather roads can be climbed throughout the year. The cool dry season is recommended for ascending the mountains of the hotter low lying regions.

Finding the way

Route finding can sometimes be difficult on the Kenya mountains for many of them are surrounded by extensive belts of natural forest, bamboo or bush. If this is dense, the only practicable route will be along cut tracks, footpaths or game trails. Game trails are not always direct. The employment of a guide will often save much valuable time on the lower slopes. Local persons, such as game guards, forest workers or herdsmen, will often act as guides for a modest reward. Once clear of the forest, on open moorland, route finding is not usually a problem, but natural forest may well go up to the summits although on many of the lower hills, such as Kamasia, the upland forest has been cleared for grazing and cultivation.

Game on the mountains

Mention of game trails leads on to the game itself. In many of the forests on Kenya's mountains, some of which are in or adjoin game parks or reserves, there is much game—not merely small buck, but giraffe, eland, lion, leopard, buffalo and rhino. Some game migrates and it may consequently be seen from time to time where it is not normally found. For instance, in 1966, elephants were seen on Suswa. In 1967 a MCK party on Namanga mountain encountered many elephants and, on the summit itself, a rhino. But only two weeks later, the elephants had migrated. Even on the Ngong hills near Nairobi, buffalo and eland are frequently to be seen, although they usually stay away from the path.

Although there is so much game, it is not ordinarily a hazard. Game moves off if given warning of the approach of people, and indeed, unless you move very quietly on the mountains you will be unlikely to see very much apart from an occasional steaming dropping. The game is there however, and caution should be exercised. If you see big game, do not attempt to approach near it. Wait till it becomes aware of your presence and moves away before continuing. On some remote mountains like Kadam, where lions abound, a game guard might be comforting for a small party. After dark, particular caution is to be exercised. The best advice about moving in the mountain forests after dark is: don't. If however you must, perhaps because of a delayed descent, give ample warning of your approach. Failure to observe this precept undoubtedly contributed to the tragedy which occurred on Mount Kenya in 1966 when a couple descending after dusk came unexpectedly upon a herd of elephant and one person was trampled to death. This is the only fatality of this kind which is known to have occurred to a mountain party in Kenya, although some people can tell tales of being delayed by buffalo or elephant which have been reluctant to move out of the path.

Apparel

The question of clothing and equipment may be mentioned here. At night the altitude makes most of the mountains cold. During the day, temperatures range from hot through pleasantly warm to cold, depending on the altitude, season and wind. For the snow mountains such as Mount Kenya, alpine clothing is evidently necessary. On some of the other higher mountains too, similar protective clothing should be in reserve. In general however, only light clothing is required with a hat, although wind may make a windbreaker useful. If there is much thorn bush to be traversed, slacks rather than shorts should be worn. A pullover for the mornings and evenings in the higher mountains will be useful. As to footwear, practice varies. Some people wear ordinary alpine climbing boots, but these are heavy and hot. A lighter boot will usually be satisfactory, cooler and more comfortable. Light canvas hockey boots are widely worn. Spanish fell boots with rubber soles are cheap, light, comfortable and afford good protection. Carry a compass and a map and a whistle. Snakes are sometimes seen on the mountains and some people carry a snake bite kit. If the route description mentions bush and forest, carry a panga for clearing and trail-blazing. The sun's rays are intense and a protective lotion should be used.

Maps

A word about maps may be useful. The most valuable general map for planning purposes is the 1:1,000,000 Safari Map of Kenya. For the approaches to the mountains the Survey of Kenya quarter-inch maps (1:250,000) will be found the most useful. For route finding on the mountains, these small-scale maps may be supplemented by maps at a scale of 1:50,000 but not all of these are contoured. References to maps are given after each route description. All of the maps listed may be obtained from the Public Map Office, Nairobi, unless otherwise indicated. A priced catalogue of maps may also be obtained from the same source.

Formalities

Most of the districts in which the mountains lie, or through which they must be approached, are Closed Districts under the provisions of the Outlying Districts Act. Before travelling in these districts permits should be obtained. Those without them may be refused entrance at road barriers or, if they are found in the district without authorisation, they may be subject to penalties. Permits are ordinarily obtainable without difficulty on application to the district or provincial administration giving the names of all members in the party and the make and registration number of their vehicles. Of the districts affected by this legislation which are of interest to mountaineers, nearly all lie in the Rift Valley Province. These districts are: Turkana, Pokot, Samburu, Elgeyo-Marakwet, Baringo, Narok and Kajiado. Permits to enter these districts may be obtained from the Provincial Commissioner, Rift Valley Province, Nakuru. The District Commissioner, Nairobi, is usually willing to issue permits for Narok and Kajiado Districts, which is convenient since the mountains in these areas are normally approached, not through Nakuru, but direct from Nairobi. For the sake of completeness it should be mentioned that the whole of the North Eastern Province (which includes Isiolo and Marsabit Districts) is closed. In the Coast Province, Lamu and Tana River Districts are also closed, but these are not of any interest to mountain climbers.

Certain formalities should be complied with before entering Mountain National Parks. At present there are three of these in Kenya, namely the Aberdares, Mount Kenya and Mount Elgon. Others may be gazetted later. For the main access roads to these parks, which are controlled, all formalities may be completed by signing in at the barriers, and paying any necessary entrance fee. For access roads not normally used by tourists, permission to enter should be obtained from the Warden, Mountain National Parks, Nyeri.

Fire bonds may be required of visitors to parts of Mount Kenya and the Aberdares at certain times of the year when the fire hazard is high. For visitors to the parks by the ordinary tourist roads, these are completed at barriers on the road. For visitors to other parts—for instance the northern Aberdares for Sattima—fire bonds can be signed in the Forest Department, Kenyatta Avenue, Nairobi, or at District Forest Offices. Forest permits are also required for climbing Meru from Olkokola. These may be obtained from the District Forest Officer at Moshi.

Accommodation

In several areas there are excellent hotels which offer a good base for ascents but generally the hills are far from hotels, and the climber must therefore be self contained and prepared to camp. Since in many cases a full day on the hill is required to reach the summit, it is desirable to camp as near the roadhead as possible and if there are farm or forest roads, to use these to get as high as possible. Some of the summits can only be conveniently reached by spending a night on the mountain. For climbers frequenting the high alpine zone on Mount Kenya there are several huts belonging to the MCK. There is also a hut belonging to the Mountain Club of Uganda on the west side of Elgon. For The Elephant in the Aberdares, and for Mount Meru, permission may be obtained to use Forestry Department huts on these mountains. Elsewhere, apart from the huts on Kilimanjaro, Sabinio, and Ruwenzori, which are outside the scope of this guide, it will be necessary to bivouac or to camp if a night on the mountain is called for.

Finally, bear in mind that many of Kenya's mountains are large, wild and remote. It is as well to climb them in company and to leave behind details of your plans.

2. The Exploration
of the East African Mountains

The pleasures of climbing mountains are, for many mountaineers, equalled only by the vicarious enjoyment to be derived from reading about mountain exploration and climbing. The literature of mountaineering in East Africa, although not so extensive as that for some other important mountain areas is nevertheless considerable. But it relates mainly to the three great snow mountains—Ruwenzori, Kenya and Kilimanjaro. The history of their first sighting by Europeans and of their subsequent exploration and climbing is a fascinating record.

Kilimanjaro was the first of the three great mountains to be seen by Europeans, and it was the first to be explored and climbed. It was the missionary, Rebmann, who first sighted the mountain on 11th May 1848. He recorded this remarkable discovery in the *Church Missionary Intelligencer* of May 1849 but was ridiculed by Cooley and other pundits of the day who refused to believe that snow might lie so close to the equator. However, British travellers pushing westward into East Africa soon confirmed that Kilimanjaro indeed existed and bore a mantle of snow, although it was not until 1862-3 that attempts were made to set foot on the higher slopes of the mountain. In that season, Baron von der Decken accompanied by Otto Kersten, reached a height of about 14,000 ft. and their surveyor estimated the height of the peak at 22,814 ft. The missionary Charles New from the Methodist mission at Ribe near Mombasa, was the first to reach snow on the saddle, in 1867. Other visits were made to Kilimanjaro by G. A. Fischer in 1883, by Sir Harry Johnston in 1884 who succeeded in reaching over 16,000 ft., and by Count Teleki and von Höhnel in 1887. In 1887 Hans Meyer reached 18,000 ft. and in the following year, with the guide Ludwig Purtscheller of Salzburg, he attained the summit of Kibo. He also climbed one of the lower summits of Mawenzi, the sister peak of Kibo, but the highest summit of Mawenzi was not climbed until 1912, by Oehler and Klute.

Soon after the sighting of the snows of Kilimanjaro, Johann Krapf, Rebmann's colleague, claimed to have seen the glaciers of Mount Kenya, on 3rd December 1849, from Kitui, nearly a hundred miles away. His claim too, was derided and it was not until much later, in 1883, that it was confirmed by the Scottish explorer, Joseph Thomson who passed close to Mount Kenya on his way across the Laikipia plateau. Count Teleki's expedition of 1887 was the first to set foot on the mountain itself, and succeeded in reaching a height of about 14,000 ft., well up on the moorland zone on the south-western slopes of the mountain. Two or three years later an expedition led by Capt. F. G. Dundas and including Bird Thompson and C. W. Hobley, made an attempt on the southern slopes but failed to penetrate the forest belt. In 1893 J. W. Gregory ascended the glacier zone to about 15,500 ft. In 1896 George Kolb reached the moorland from the east and in 1899, H. J. Mackinder with the two Courmayeur guides, Joseph Brocherel and César Ollier, succeeded in climbing Batian, the highest summit. Much exploration was done after the first world war, but it was not until 1929 that P. Wyn Harris and Eric Shipton ascended Nelion peak for the first time, and also made the second ascent of Batian.

Although the existence of the Ruwenzori range was not proved to the outside world until 1888, the presence of snow mountains in Africa was suspected over

two thousand years ago. In the second century, Ptolemy inscribed on his map the *Montes Lunae*, from whose waters flowed the great lakes that fed the Nile. The Ruwenzori range is generally identified with these legendary Mountains of the Moon, although it has been suggested by O.G.S. Crawford that they really lay in Abyssinia. Soon after Kenya and Kilimanjaro were first seen, it was suggested that those must be the Mountains of the Moon of antiquity, but Speke and Baker showed that the isolated mountains of Kenya and Kilimanjaro were in fact separated from the Nile basin by the eastern branch of the Great Rift Valley. In 1858 Speke discovered Lake Victoria Nyanza and in 1862 he reached the Ripon Falls where the Nile issues from the lake to commence its journey to the Mediterranean. In 1864 Baker reached Lake Albert and from its southern end saw a range veiled in mist. He was in fact looking at the northern end of the Ruwenzori range but the mists hid the snow. Nearly a quarter of a century was to pass before the snows were first seen. Stanley had been commissioned to rescue Emin Pasha, Governor of the Equatoria Province of Sudan, who had been cut off by the Mahdist rising. The snows of Ruwenzori were first seen on April 20th 1888, by two members of Stanley's expedition, Parks and Mounteney-Jephson, from near the shores of Lake Albert. Stanley called the range "Runsori". According to R. M. Bere, this word means the place where the rains come from.

Eighteen years passed after the identification of the Ruwenzori before the major summits were scaled. Many unsuccessful attempts were made. Among these may be mentioned that of Johnston who in 1900 reached a height of about 15,000 ft. Impenetrable vegetation, perennial rain or mist proved formidable obstacles. In 1906, however, the range was at last thoroughly explored by the expedition of the Duke of the Abruzzi. In the course of this expedition, which was mounted on the grand scale, all of the major summits were climbed, mapped and photographed. The ascent of the highest peak, Margherita, was not repeated until 1927, when it was climbed by Humphreys in the course of his remarkable expeditions.

Thus the history of the European exploration of the greater East African mountains is clear and it has been recounted on many occasions. For most of the lesser mountains however, ascents were for the most part incidental to some scientific or administrative pursuit and the record is scattered in the works of geographers, geologists, surveyors and others. For most of the early travellers moreover, the mountains were obstacles to be circumvented rather than climbed. And while it is tolerably certain that the peaks of the three great snow mountains had never before been climbed, the same cannot be said of many of the lesser peaks. It is certain that many of these would have been climbed by indigenous pastoralists and hunters, although in some cases, as with Lengai, this would be very unlikely; and sometimes taboos operated which were powerful enough to prevent Africans from accompanying Europeans even for substantial reward. But in many other cases the mountains clearly provided herbage and were often well populated by virtue of their favourable rainfall. The Taita hills come into this category and, like others, they were the source both of water and food for early caravans.

Some of the hills along the Mombasa road to Voi are spectacular, although they are not particularly high. They and the Taita hills were visited by many early travellers including von der Decken, Krapf and Rebmann, Charles New, and Thomson. Rebmann travelled by the Ndara hills (the Sagala Hills) as early as 1847. In October of that year he wished to climb to the summit of Kadiaro (Kisigau), but was refused permission on the pretext that, as he was wearing shoes, he would certainly fall. He was clearly suspected of being a spy. In the following May he climbed a small peak in the Taita hills from Chawia. It was in the course of his travels in the Taita hills that Rebmann first glimpsed the snows of Kilimanjaro. New climbed the south-west shoulder of Kisigau (5,383 ft.) in July 1863 and commented: "Never did I perform a harder three hours' task . . . ." The dome of Kisigau, surrounded by its perpendicular cliffs, reminded him of St. Paul's Cathedral. New also visited the Taita Hills beyond Voi and climbed a spur of Bura (Vuria). He also climbed to the top of Muarimba (Mairimba)—3,716 ft.—south of the Voi-Taveta road.

In 1883 J. J. Thomson climbed to the summit of Ndara (Mrumunyi). It took him a stiff three hours. He then made his way to Bura mountain and reached a valley running deep into the mountain "to the base of the commanding dome of Kilima Kibomu . . . An attempt to ascend to the top of Mount Kibomu failed through the stupidity of our guide, who took us the wrong road, and landed me finally at the bottom of a steep precipice, 1,000 ft. from the top".

Many of the mountains of Kenya lie in the vast extent of country over which the Maasai held sway in the nineteenth century. For a long time the fearsome reputation of this tribe kept Europeans out of their territories. Nevertheless, information on the geography of their territory was not wholly lacking. From the mid-eighteenth century, Arab and Swahili traders sent caravans into the interior and they were well acquainted with the main facts of its geography. For the outside world, one of the earliest sources of information on Maasailand was the data collected by Clemens Denhardt of Lamu and by T. Wakefield of Mombasa. They carefully recorded the itineraries of a large number of such traders, and on their basis prepared maps which marked every important lake, river and mountain in Maasailand—although not always accurately—before a single European had set foot in the interior. Jackson, incidentally, believed that the terrors and dangers of entering Maasailand had been purposely and grossly exaggerated by early traders with the object of keeping their happy hunting grounds free of poachers. He himself refused to pay the customary *hongo* or tribute, and the result was most satisfactory.

Fischer was the first European to enter Maasailand. He entered the Rift Valley in 1883 from what is now Tanzania and followed it northward past Lengai, which was then steaming. He then continued along the western shores of Lake Natron, passed near Longonot and discovered Fischer's tower in Hell's Gate near Naivasha, before he was forced to turn back for lack of food.

Later in the same year, J. J. Thomson continued the exploration of the Rift Valley farther north. In the course of his expedition he climbed or attempted several mountains. His ascents around Taita have been mentioned already. In August, on his way north, he climbed a mountain which he called Donyo Erok la Matumbato. This mountain, whose height he put at 6,000 ft., was presumably Namanga mountain and it seems likely that he climbed the accessible shoulder visible from the road, which is about that height. In September 1883 he made the first recorded attempt on Longonot, but only succeeded in reaching a height of 8,300 ft. on the crater rim. The ascent was made in good spirits to the accompaniment of shouts of *Excelsior* in Ki-swahili. Of the crater rim he records: "So sharp was the edge of this marvellous crater that I literally sat astride on it, with one leg dangling over the abyss internally, and the other down the side of the mountain". From the crater rim: "We hastily retraced our steps for the sun had almost set and we knew only too well that there were lions as well as Maasai in

8

the path". Some days later he decided to ascend Eburu, and, taking eight men, he set off "for this dangerous trip". He reached the crater lake and started to climb the mountain, but "was prevented from ascending it by the threatening appearance of the sky". Thomson was clearly no peak-bagger.

During 1887-8 the important expedition of Teleki added much to the knowledge of the northern end of the Rift Valley. But although several smaller ranges of mountains were crossed or skirted, and some larger ones, such as Nyiro were visited, the main interest of the expedition from the standpoint of mountain exploration lies in its penetration, for the first time, of Mount Kenya to a height of 14,000 ft., an achievement which has already been noted. The expedition also attempted to climb Mount Meru, but torrential rain forced them to give up hope of getting to the top.

Of the larger East African mountains below the snow line, one of the most interesting is Mount Elgon which lies on the borders of Kenya and Uganda. The first European to see Elgon may have been Stanley who called it Masaba, but there is considerable doubt as to whether his identification was correct. J. J. Thomson later explored the caves on the flanks of the mountain. The summit itself was first climbed in February 1890 by F. Jackson (later Governor of Uganda and of Kenya), E. W. Gedge and James Martin. Martin was a former Maltese sail-maker who had accompanied Thomson through Maasailand. He subsequently became H. M. Collector in Baringo and was the first European encountered in East Africa by Delamere and Atkinson on their journey in from the north.

According to Jackson's book, their ascent of Mount Elgon was not really intended. When they left Save, or Sebei, (the present Kapchorwa) on the northern slopes of the mountain, they had no intention of attempting to cross the mountain. They had engaged guides to take them to Mangikas by a road circling the eastern side of the mountain, but on the way they encountered traces of Nandi raiders. Possibly the guides may have misunderstood their instructions, or being ignorant of the use of fire-arms, they may have considered it advisable for the party not to run the risk of encountering the raiders. Whatever the explanation, Jackson did not discover the mistake until they were well on the way and they decided to continue. Gedge's diary, however, suggests that they did in fact start out with the definite intention of climbing the mountain.

Jackson commented on his ascent thus:
> *"I am not a mountain-climbing enthusiast, and cannot recall a moment of pleasurable feeling during that long, wearisome and monotonous journey to the top of Mount Elgon; the fact that I was one of the first to accomplish it 'left me cold' in more senses than one. All I claim, and I may even stand out alone in that respect, perhaps for centuries, is that I was the first white man who spent his thirtieth birthday in the crater".*

The crater itself, however, with its spectacular views did not disappoint him.
> *"It was worth all the toil and trouble of going up and having a peep into it, but I would not do it again with four hundred odd men".*

They reached the summit on February 17th and by boiling point thermometer determined the height at 14,192 ft. On the following day they climbed the highest peak on the south side which Gedge determined at 14,094 ft. Having done this they departed for the fleshpots of Kavirondo.

There is some doubt as to which peak the expedition climbed on February 17th. The peak they climbed on the eighteenth however, was, probably Kiongo. Thomas and Lindsell convincingly argue that they did not, in any case, go near the summit which today bears Jackson's name.

In 1891 the decision was taken by the Imperial British East African Trading Company to make a preliminary survey of a route for a railway from Mombasa to the Victoria Nyanza. Major J. R. L. Macdonald, R. E., was selected as Chief Engineer. His second in command was Capt. J. W. Pringle, R. E. In the course of the survey the two climbed a number of smaller hills, and to Macdonald we owe a delightful account of an ascent of the prominent rocky mountain, Nzoi (Nzaui) which lies to the north of Emali. Well known to early explorers, and aptly described by Lugard as "the massive sentinel that guards the gate to the heart of Africa", Nzaui is today a popular belvedere for climbers. For the idle, a road from the north winds up virtually to the summit from which the views over the precipices to the surrounding countryside and to Kilimanjaro are quite spectacular. The ambitious can toy with the ascent of the southern rock faces, which have not so far been climbed.

Macdonald reached Nzoi in February 1892:

> "The natives told us there was only one possible track from this side, and pointed out what appeared from the camp a narrow crack running up the stupendous cliffs at an angle of 45° or more; they assured us that we must face this, or else make a detour of one day's journey north or east. They were willing enough to point out the path or track from below, but when we asked for guides we found that superstitious fears held them back. A spirit of exceptional powers was supposed to reside in this lofty peak, and they feared to provoke him by intruding on his barren crags. At last, after a good deal of talk and a handsome present, two daring men who evidently thought we were relations of the dread spirit of Nzoi, agreed to accompany us. The summit of the peak was 2,400 ft. above the camp. For the first thousand feet the ascent was over a steep slope strewn with enormous boulders, but above this rose sheer precipices of twelve to fourteen hundred feet. We made an early start, and after surmounting the first slope were glad to rest in a cool cave at the foot of the precipice. We could now see the line we had to take. A more or less broken ledge ran up the face of the precipice at a steep angle; at some places it gave barely foothold, and at others it opened to a width of thirty feet. At one spot we could see that the ledge ceased, and the climber would have to work along the face of the precipice as best he could, by means of little projections or weather-worn footholds. In spite of these difficulties, however, the path looked practicable."

With Pringle and a few men to carry the theodolite, the ascent was commenced. An encounter with a swarm of angry bees delayed them, but eventually they reached the top of the cliff to find themselves on a flat ridge, waist deep in genuine bracken. From this point they easily reached the summit to be rewarded by:

> "a view that could not readily be surpassed. At our feet lay the camp, looking small and insignificant, with Lilliputian inhabitants; beyond, amidst the light-green gardens and fields wound the Nzoi river like a silver thread; while the valley was enclosed by a wooded range, on the north side of which, broken by a mass of rocky mountains, stretched a broad, open expanse of grass towards the Kapote (Kaputiei) steppes. To the south-west was the

forest region we had lately crossed, with Bwinzau standing out clear and distinct, and the Kyulu (Chyulu) Hills becoming blue in the distance. Beyond these again, half hidden in horizontal clouds, gilded with the level rays of the afternoon sun, beautiful as ever, and dwarfing in its gigantic proportions all the intermediate hills, stood out the great snowy dome of Kilimanjaro":

They began the descent, but waited near the bee-cave until after sunset. When assured that the bees had retired for the night they continued the descent, eventually reaching the camp after eleven.

Towards the end of the same year, J. W. Gregory, a member of the Alpine Club and at that time a geologist at the British Museum, arrived in East Africa as a member of an expedition which collapsed. Determined not to return to England without something to show for his journey, he organised his own expedition from the coast to the Rift Valley, in the course of which he got as far north as Lake Baringo. He was the only European in his party, and was quite unacquainted with the country or the inhabitants; but despite these handicaps he accomplished a great deal and produced a classical study of the Great Rift Valley. In the course of his investigations, as already pointed out, he attained a height of some 15,500 ft. on Mount Kenya. He spent some time on the Lewis glacier and climbed Mount Höhnel. On his way up from the coast he climbed a number of lesser hills. Unlike Thomson, he appears to have believed in getting to the top.

One of his first ascents was of Mount Ndi or Mbololi, which he wrongly assumed to be the highest mountain of the Teita group. This he undertook on March 30th, 1893.

"At daybreak next morning I started from camp with a couple of the Askari; we followed the course of a small stream, which came plunging down the mountain side in a series of picturesque cascades. To force a way straight up the slope was impossible, owing to the denseness of the vegetation. We tried to do so, but were soon glad to take advantage of a path which wound up the face of the mountain to some Taita villages on the upper slopes. The path was well planned for security; it was arranged to lead occasionally across the face of an almost vertical cliff, where the foothold was reduced to a few knobs, or a narrow ledge of rock. Many of the tracks in the Alps which are dignified with the name of 'mauvais pas' are safe in comparison with these. That the natives can pass along them with heavy loads of food on their heads is a great testimony to their sureness of foot and steadiness of nerve. At first I thought that these rock-traverses were only short cuts, and that the main path ran elsewhere. But it was not so; the arrangement has been planned to enable the natives to keep their mountain fastnesses safe from the marauding Masai, who could not force them if defended from above by the natives with boulders, and with bows and poisoned arrows. After a gentle ramble for two hours up the hillside, stopping here and there on the way to collect, we reached the meadows and valleys, in which are situated the villages and shambas of the Wa-taita. Only a few months previously the natives had quarrelled with a European caravan; they had dammed up the stream, and so cut off the water supply from the camp below. For this they had been so severely punished that I felt doubtful as to my reception. I found them, however, in a most friendly mood. They loaded my two men with presents of cobs of green maize, pumpkins, and sugar cane, and gave me a few eggs. The terrace beside the village commanded a good view of the upper

part of the ridge, and I was thus able to decide on the best route to the summit. The headman of the village lent me two men as guides. A sharp walk soon brought us to the ridge, and we went southward along it, until at half past eleven we reached the margin of the clump of trees upon the summit. The guides and my own men refused to go farther, as they said the wood was the abode of evil spirits and they dared not enter. I left them to light a fire, while I pushed on through the shrubs alone. This however, was a waste of time, except in so far as it satisfied my climbing conscience. There was no view from the summit, and I had to make my sketches and observations from the edge of the wood. We boiled the water for the thermometers, and obtained data from which I subsequently calculated the altitude at 5,640 ft".

Continuing on his way to the interior, he climbed Nzaui in early April, as well as several other minor hills, such as Etwa in the Kilungu hills, Tututha and Givoni, before making his way to Machakos and Fort Smith and descending into the Rift Valley. From his camp at the foot of the escarpment he ascended a mountain he refers to as Doenyo Nyuki, which was probably Mount Margaret. Two days later he camped at the foot of Longonot and, knowing that the summit had not been ascended, resolved to attempt the ascent.

"It was very cold in the morning, and so wet and cloudy that it was eight o'clock before we were able to start ... A sharp scramble of an hour and a half brought us to the rim of the crater, which at the point where we reached it has been worn by zebras into a broad cinder track. The floor of the crater is a large and fairly level plain, covered with acacia scrub; the walls are usually precipitous, but a descent could easily be made on the southern side. The great surprise was the discovery of a large steam vent on the inner face of the north wall of the crater ... The actual summit of the mountain is on the western side, and is 1,800' higher than the rim of the crater at the point where we reached it. We started for it along the northern wall. At first the way was easy, but as the edge of the crater rose, it became jagged and densely covered with scrub. To avoid some of the teeth, we worked across the inner face of the crater. After a weary scramble of an hour and three quarters we reached the foot of the final pinnacle. A narrow sharp ridge of volcanic ash led up to it. This was very slippery, and it sloped rapidly down on either side to cliffs of such height, that the two Zanzibaris refused to traverse it. I cut steps across it and reached the dense bush that covered the summit. For a moment I doubted whether after all I should be able to force a way through the bush, for the foothold was precarious, and a slip would have been easy and disastrous. To return, however, when so near the summit was not to be thought of, so I hewed a way through the scrub with a sword bayonet. After sketching the surrounding country from the summit I returned to the men and we boiled the thermometers, thus obtaining data which indicate for the highest pinnacle a height of 9,350 feet. We then raced back to camp. Civilisation proved its superiority to nature, for thanks to boots and an alpenstock I arrived there at 2.15, an hour before the men."

From his later camp at Kariandusi, Gregory climbed one of the Dondole mountains, christening it Kilima Meza, and, on the way to Baringo, a peak he called Equator Peak (6,150 ft.) before crossing Laikipia. The Maasai had earlier prevented Thomson from crossing the Ewaso Nyiro. Although four years later, Count Teleki marched across Laikipia by the main Swahili trade route without interference, his force was very powerful. In 1889/90 Karl Peters allegedly had to fight his way across Laikipia. This history was known to Gregory and it was enough to persuade him to choose a new route in an attempt to avoid meeting the dreaded Maasai. In this he was successful.

Many of the lesser mountains of East Africa have carried pastoral populations for as long as we have records and some, as in the Taita Hills, also had extensive cultivations which provided supplies to early caravans. In the arid northern district of Kenya, Marsabit Mountain was naturally visited by early travellers coming from the north, affording as it did water and other supplies. The earliest description of the mountain is that of Donaldson Smith who seems to have been the first European to see it. He records an ascent made in September 1893.

> "We left the Rendile on September the 9th, with our water barrels well filled, as we were told that the next water which could be obtained was on top of Marsabit. On the second day we commenced to ascend the mountain, but we did not reach the top until after three marches. According to European ideas, nothing could be more charming than this Marsabit. Surrounded by a large forest, and lying on the top of the mountain, is a lake a mile square, clear and deep. The jagged walls of the crater form a semicircle about it, while from another side a broad road leads from the forest to the open meadows beyond. The atmosphere is moist and cool. In the early morning dense clouds are swept along by invigorating blasts of cold air, combining with the dew of night to freshen up the plants and trees. Outside the forest the view is superb. For five miles you see a series of green meadows sloping gradually downward, on which are grazing many sheep and goats; while far off to the west, beyond the yellow plain, rises rugged Kulal, and a still greater mountain below it—Mt. Njyiro. Living on Marsabit are many Maasai, enjoying themselves in the possession of large flocks of sheep and goats. In the two days that we remained at Marsabit, Dodson and I collected many rare specimens of birds and mammals, though we could catch no fish whatsoever in the lake. I also had some good sport with elephant."

When Delamere arrived a few years later in the course of his 1896/7 expedition, the Samburu were in possession of the mountain. It still swarmed with elephant. Atkinson, Delamere's companion, shot twenty-one elephants in twenty-one days.

At about the time Gregory was undertaking his explorations, the Chanler expedition was working its way across the Nyambeni range. However, they did not climb any of the main summits although they reached a height of 7,200 ft.

By the end of the nineteenth century, the initial exploration phase conducted by expeditions making large sweeps through often unknown country was over although much detailed work remained to be done, and it was still possible for new routes to be found. In the course of the First Nandi Expedition of 1895, S. Vandeleur found a short cut to Lake Victoria which saved 80-100 miles and, in doing so, climbed what was clearly Timboroa (9,489 ft.). Scientific expeditions continued to arrive from overseas, but their work became much more intensive. The work of detailed mapping was initially undertaken in connection with boundary delimitation, railway surveys, lake surveys, and settlement, and, later by the Survey and Geological Departments. Thus, Suswa was climbed in October 1897 by F. Hall with J. Blackett and Welby in the course of the Uganda Railway Survey. Mount Blackett (a spur of the Mau, south-west of Mau Summit—8,580 ft.) was climbed by Blackett in September 1898. B. Whitehouse climbed many of the lakeside hills from Mohoru to Sio in 1900. In the course of work for the Anglo-German Boundary Commission of 1902-4, G. E. Smith's party climbed Gwasi (partially, to 6,399 ft). Oldoinyo Sambu (6,383 ft.), Shombole (partially, to 4,850 ft.), and Oldoinyo Erok (8,386 ft.). The record of the ascents undertaken for these purposes is mainly locked up in inaccessible field reports and diaries. Some, however, were published.

Among such published reports is an account of an ascent of Kulal, first climbed in 1903 by P. Maud in connection with the delimitation of the border between Abyssinia and British East Africa. He describes the ascent of this spectacular mountain in undramatic terms.

> *"Nearing the south end of the lake, we got into very bad stony ground. On Mount Kulal were another section of Lokkobb. They were very shy, but eventually I got on terms with them, and, during a long conversation conducted by signs, I was able to make a small vocabulary of their language. They made me a present of a bullock, and I gave them clasp knives and beads in return. In the evening they showed us a good track down the mountain."*

Maud also visited other mountains in the neighbourhood, one group of which he christened the Eland Range.

From the middle of the last decade of the nineteenth century until the beginning of the First World War, much scientific investigation was undertaken by German scientists on the volcanoes and highlands of German East Africa. In the course of these exhaustive studies, some of which were not published until 1940, a number of ascents of important mountains were made. In 1894, Oscar Neumann got to within five hundred feet of the summit of Lengai. During the same journey, Neumann ascended to the Loita mountains from below Nguruman and, on his way back to the coast, he crossed the Chyulu range. According to Hobley, Kaiser ascended the summit of Lengai during the Schöller expedition of 1898, but Uhlig states that the first ascent to the summit by himself, Jaeger and Gunzert took place during his expedition, on 4th Sept. 1904.

Other ascents made by the German geographers which relate to mountains outside the area covered by this guide, include Gurui, Monduli, Loolmasin, and of course, Jaeger Summit. Ngorongoro crater was first seen by Oscar Baumann in 1892. Reck later climbed Kitumbeine.

The impressive mass of Meru was first climbed by Jaeger in 1904. Other early recorded ascents of Meru are by A. L. Henneker Gotley in January 1926 via Nandunguro Ravine, and by Carl Brinkman and Ulrich Trappe from Momella in January 1929. T. A. Barns was the first British traveller to visit and describe the Great Craterland, in 1920, but he does not appear to have climbed (except to the rim of Ngorongoro), although he did make an excursion to Lengai.

Bearing in mind the difficulties of access and cost, it is perhaps not surprising that even the greater mountains of East Africa did not attract more climbers in the early days of European interest—not even the Ruwenzori, of which Douglas Freshfield remarked: "You may be familiar with the Alps and the Caucasus, the Himalaya and the Rockies, but if you have not explored Ruwenzori you still have something wonderful to see and do". Nevertheless, local residents, priests, farmers, officials, sometimes made ascents of the more accessible mountains for other than purely professional reasons. There is an interesting record of an ascent in 1907 of the Kinangop by a party led by Père Fillipo Perli from the Consolata Mission at Tuso. A cross was erected on the summit and mass was celebrated. Although the summit of the Kinangop is an airy alpine scramble, it is uncertain whether this was a first ascent. The Aberdare range itself, of course, has long been a means of access from the Rift Valley to Kikuyuland and there is much evidence of prehistoric travel and trade along trans-montane trackways.

The tradition of District Commissioners undertaking exploratory work as a part of their varied duties was also strong and has resulted in some records of mountain ascents. G. Archer, of Archer's Post fame, undertook a topographical survey around 1911 in the course of which he climbed the south summit of Kulal. In 1921 the legendary Baron Eric von Otter—"Bwana Risasi Moja"—ascended Ngithigerr. In 1923, J. G. Hamilton Ross ascended Sekerr. Kadam was also ascended by a local D.C., Preston, in 1931, but it may earlier have been climbed by the Krenkel expedition of 1911/13.

In the literary tradition and wholly charming are the writings of E.A.T. Dutton on Mount Kenya, and of Vivienne de Watteville. In 1928 and 1929, some years after the tragedy recorded in *Out in the Blue*, Miss de Watteville spent a season in Kenya, staying at Selengai and Namanga, and concluding with a lengthy stay on Mount Kenya. Her ascent to the mountain commenced, as was usual in those days, from Chogoria and she based herself on Urumandi Hut. Her visit to the Curling Pond, where she found the hut destroyed, coincided with the famous ascent of Batian and Nelion by Harris, Shipton and Sommerfelt.

From a camp at Namanga she had some months earlier climbed Ol Donyo Orok, meeting several rhino on the way. The whole trip took 16 hours. Her feelings on climbing that mountain have certainly been echoed by many later climbers.

> *"Then suddenly, toiling upwards through trees and creepers, I came out onto an open crest, and there before me, lifting its head above the forest, was the bare, gray summit. It might have been three hours away and it might have been thirty; all depended upon what lay between those intervening ridges suffocating under the tangled green barriers of forest. But to the eye it looked attainable, and the more I looked, the more it lured me on".*

And so, despite discouragement from her guides, this formidable woman continued up through the forest, through the heath, across the meadows carpeted with wild flowers, until at last, after photographing a rhino and being charged by it, she reached the summit and built a cairn on the middle of three summits.

Shortly after this, she climbed Longido to its prominent rock summit. Deciding correctly that the shoulder beyond the col was higher, she went on to climb that as well, once more being charged by a rhino on the way. She got back to her camp at 10 p.m. after having left very early in the morning. Certainly de Watteville's ascent of Longido was not the first. On the very summit of the rock peak, her guide showed her a branch that had been cut through with a knife. Longido is likely to have been ascended during the Anglo-German hostilities of 1914, if not earlier by the German scientific expeditions.

On the fringes of East Africa, and strictly outside the scope of this survey, are the Virunga or Bufumbira mountains, a group of eight volcanoes, some still active, which lie in the Congo and on the south-western borders of Uganda. Speke appears to have been the first white man to see and report on these volcanoes, in 1861. The first party to attempt the ascent of Mikeno (14,600 ft.) was that of the Duke of Mecklenburg which, in 1908 reached a height of about 13,000 ft. The peak was ascended completely in August 1927 by Père van Hoef and his party from the White Fathers Mission at Lulenga. Nyamlagira and Nyiragongo were first visited in 1894 by Count von Götzen, the European explorer and discoverer of Lake Kivu. He accomplished the first ascent of Nyiragongo, the higher of the two, and pronounced the volcano to be in full activity. The Duke of Mecklenburg also visited the peak in 1909. During 1931-8, Col. Hoier, warden of the Albert National Park, kept a watch on the volcano, in the course of which he made 150 ascents. The grave of Carl Akeley, the American scientist and conservationist lies on the saddle below Mikeno. L. Denman, the climber who attempted Everest alone, is alleged to be the first European to have scaled all eight volcanoes.

All of Kenya's mountains have by now been mapped and photographed. For most, the existence of survey beacons on their summits also bears witness to their ascent. There are however, still some remote tops, for example in the Mathews range, of which no record of an ascent is known. Those with a taste for exploration may thus still find scope for putting a foot where no man has been before—and left a record. For those with a taste for history there are certainly interesting narratives of ascents of some of the major peaks to be found in archives and diaries. A detailed history of the exploration of the Kenya mountains—as indeed of the East African mountains—and a full survey of their literature—remains to be written.

3. Elgon—Karamoja

1. MOUNT ELGON, 14,178 ft.
(Maasai—Oldoinyo Ilgoon—meaning mountain shaped like breasts.)

Mount Elgon is a vast extinct volcano situated on the Kenya-Uganda border. The main attraction of Elgon is its fine open walking, moorland scenery and long views. The diameter of the base of the mountain is about 80 miles, and of the summit crater about 4 miles. The crater is roughly circular and consists of a series of peaks of around 14,000 ft. There are some cliffs in the crater area, but none of them, with the possible exception of Koitoboss peak on the Kitale side, is very large or provides any worthwhile climbing. The paths on the main routes are good, the going easy (unless it is very wet), open and free of vegetation, and not particularly steep except on one of the lower sections. There is no permanent snow, although seasonal snow sometimes lies in the crater for a short time. The crater can be surprisingly cold at times, but otherwise the temperature is what one would expect according to altitude. Elgon can be climbed at any time of the year, but the months of heaviest rain, the end of April and May, August and September should be avoided if possible. In February the views are often bad due to grass burning.

Stanley was possibly the first European to see the mountain in 1875. The first European to visit it, in 1883, was J. J. Thomson who discovered and explored the caves on the southern slopes of the mountain inhabited by the El Kony clan of the Maasai. The Maasai name for the mountain is Oldoinyo Ilgoon which means mountain shaped like breasts. The clan name is derived from this. The first recorded ascent was by Jackson and Gedge in February 1890. There is some doubt as to which were the two summits they visited, but it seems clear that the summit now known by Jackson's name was not one of these.

Approach: There are two main methods of approach: one from Mbale in Uganda which has the advantage of a Club hut on the Uganda side of the mountain, and the other from Kitale, where there is a track up to 10,000 ft. A second route in Kenya goes from Kimilili, from which a track climbs high up the southern flanks of the mountain. The mountain can also be approached from Uganda by other routes; from the north (Kaburoron, Sipi or Bulago), and from the South (Bulucheke). The permission and the advice of the District Commissioner Sebei should be sought for the northern routes, and of the D.C. Bugisu for the Bulucheke route.

1. From Mbale

Approach: Drive to Bumagabula, about 25 miles. Follow the Soroti road out of Mbale for 4 miles, turn right to Buwalasi and follow the road to Budadiri (Nakiwondwe). In Budadiri bear right, after which take the first turn left. After this the first fork to the right leads to the Bumasifwa sub-county headquarters where there is an unfurnished rest camp which can be booked through the District Commissioner, Bugisu (charge Shs. 6 per night; water and wood provided). The left fork leads on up to Bumagabula up a steep hill, which may not be passable if wet, and where the porters are normally found (5,500 ft.).

Route: The path from here is 5-6 hours to the hut belonging to the Mountain Club of Uganda at Sasa (10,600 ft.). From there it is 4-5 hours to Jackson's Summit, the nearest of the summits, which does not give a view into the crater, and 5-6 hours to Wagagai, the highest summit on the crater rim.

The Sasa hut is a uniport hut. It has a tiled floor, and contains no equipment or bunks. The hut is by a stream, and there is a good firewood supply. It is not locked. Beside it is a shelter used by the porters.

The Ladkin hut which used to be in the crater has now been totally destroyed by local thieves, and tents are needed for a visit to the crater.

The minimum expedition on Elgon by this route is two days, i.e. one night at Sasa hut, which allows time to reach Jackson's Summit, or possibly Wagagai on the second day and return to roadhead. This, however, means a very long day and three or four days is preferable, and a week can enjoyably be spent exploring the mountain.

The Sasa Hut can be booked through the Hut and Equipment Secretary, M.C.U.

Fees are Shs. 1 for members and members of reciprocating clubs, and Shs. 2 for non-members. A deposit in advance for the full value of hut fees is payable before confirmation of bookings. Please make certain to leave the hut clean and burn or bury rubbish.

No medical supplies are kept in the hut. The nearest dispensary is at Budadiri, and the nearest hospital in Mbale.

Porters are arranged through the District Commissioner, Bugisu, who requires at least two weeks' notice in order that the chief at Bumasifwa can be informed and asked to arrange for the porters to be ready. Headmen are also available, and are normally taken when more than a small number of porters is being taken, or when a guide to Jackson's Summit, or Wagagai is required. If a reasonably early start is made, the porters can carry to the Sasa Hut and return on the same day. If a late start is made (parties should not leave later than 1.00 p.m.) and the porters have to sleep at Sasa they will require food, and it is advisable to provide them with a few cheap blankets. At Sasa they sleep in a separate shelter near the hut.

It has been very difficult in recent years to keep to fixed wages, and porters have often been difficult to satisfy, and sometimes difficult to obtain. A fair wage is felt to be Shs. 7 which is about the present minimum, and Shs. 10 is sometimes asked.

2. From Kitale
(240 miles from Nairobi on fast roads).

Approach: Take the Endebess road and cross three rivers north of Endebess on the North Elgon road, and take a road up to the left leading to Tweedie's farm and the Suam Sawmills. In dry weather an ordinary car can reach the end of the forest track at 10,000 ft. approximately; in wet weather a Land Rover is definitely necessary. After passing two turnings to the left to a forest station and a village, take a turning left marked "Moorland Track". The end of this is 14 miles from the main road. There is a good camping site and firewood, but no water.

Route: From the end of the track it is 4-5 hours to Koitoboss peak or the crater rim and 2-2½ hours down. There is a suitable camp site and water half an hour short of the crater rim on the path which then continues over into the crater and across to the Uganda side. Parties do not usually take porters on this route, but the District Commissioner, Kitale, may be able to obtain them.

3. From Kimilili

Approach: Follow the road to Kitale for 2½ miles. Turn left for Kapsakwony (4 miles on). At Kapsakwony turn left for D.C.'s camp (1½ miles). Continue for a further 13 miles to Laboot. From here the track continues and may be followed for as much as another five miles.

Route: From the end of the track a path takes one to Sudek, from which Lower Elgon (14,410 ft.) (survey pillar) may be attained. Time: 3 hours if the track is passable to the end.

Maps
1:250,000 Mbale shows Uganda side.
1:250,000 Kapenguria shows Kenya side.
1:50,000 Kenya Sheet 74/111 shows Kenya side and summit area.
1:50,000 Uganda Sheet 74/W/IV shows Uganda side.

2. KADAM (Debasien), 10,067 ft.

Kadam, which is also called Debasien by certain tribes in the area, is an eroded volcano rising to 10,067 ft., and situated in the southern part of Karamoja District in Eastern Uganda, mid-way between Mt. Elgon and Mt. Moroto. The lower slopes are thickly forested and rise from the dry thorny savannah of the surrounding plain. The basic structure is of a long ridge between the two main peaks, Obda to the West and Tebtho to the East, and a very complicated series of subsidiary ridges radiating from them. The higher parts of the mountain are characterised by steep lava cliffs, and thick heather vegetation. The mountain provides a good walking expedition of 2-3 days in very attractive scenery. Johnston remarked of the mountain, "So far as outline goes, I think Debasien is the most beautiful mountain in Central Africa". Some rock climbing has been done on Tebtho and there are considerable possibilities for exploring new routes of approach to the peaks though communications to the starting points are difficult. It is a dry mountain and there are very few streams or waterholes. For this reason alone a guide is necessary. The first recorded ascent was in 1931 by Preston, a local D.C. Kadam was visited and possibly climbed by the Krenkel expedition of 1911/12.

Approach: From *Uganda* the mountain can be approached by the watershed road from Mbale via Chepsikunya to Moroto. Beyond Namalu on the west of the mountain, the road traverses round the foot of it and reaches a point very close beneath Obda, before bearing away north towards Moruita. At the point where the road runs closest to the mountain there is a Geological Survey Department camp which is a convenient place to leave a car for the climb to Obda. Before starting the climb however, it is necessary to go to Moruita to advise the Jakait (Sub-County Chief) of one's intention to climb the mountain and to obtain a guide and porters if desired. Most parties in the past have started to walk from Moruita, but for Obda a 5 mile walk through the grassy plains can be avoided by starting at the Geological camp. Moruita is about 90 miles from Mbale on a good road, although the section across the Sebei plains and south of Namalu can be sticky in the rains. *From Kenya*, Moruita can be reached from Kitale via Kacheliba and Amudat (100 miles). The road is quite good in most seasons but can be impassable after rains. It is not at present necessary to obtain a letter of authority from the District Commissioner to visit Kadam, but it is advisable to inform the D.C. of one's visit, and if it is desired to arrange porters in advance it is necessary to do so through him.

The mountain can be climbed at any time of year. Views are probably better in the rainy season and there is more water on the mountain. With a guide however there is no difficulty in finding water at any time of year. The rainy season is in March, April and May and it is generally dry for the rest of the year.

Obda

Routes: Either start from Moruita and walk across the plains or start from the Geological Survey camp and walk up the valley leading from it into the forest. Follow the valley to the base of lava cliffs. Then climb the right hand (south) side of the valley and emerge on an open ridge. There is a water hole there. Then traverse south to the next ridge and follow it to the base of a sheer lava pinnacle. Descend the ridge on its south side for a few hundred feet to a large rock shelter with a water hole. This is the usual campsite and takes about 4 hours to reach. Then follow the north side of this valley for about an hour and cross to the opposite side at a rock ridge which runs across the valley. Climb steeply up through forest and grass and occasional rock steps to the crest of the ridge, which is then followed to the summit plateau. The summit is reached after about a mile of hard going through heather scrub. The ascent from the campsite and return takes about 5 hours. The return to the road takes about $2\frac{1}{2}$ hours. The climb can thus be done in 3 days of easy going and by a fit party carrying minimum loads in 2 days.

Tebtho

The usual route goes from the campsite on the Obda route straight up to the ridge between the two peaks where there is a campsite on the ridge (about half an hour after reaching it, in the direction of the summit) which is equipped with a small permanent puddle (6 hours). Next day go along the ridge to the summit. There is much giant heather and progress is slow. The summit itself is airy and to get to the very top involves two short rock pitches—a slab and a wall. It is not difficult but a rope may be useful for novices. Return to the campsite on the same day.

Tebtho has also been ascended direct by the ridge from Moruita. It is best to keep to the ridge as much as possible but a guide is necessary to ensure success on this ascent and to find water. There is a campsite with water shortly below the rock ridge which is the final stage of the climb. The ridge provides climbing on firm rock of Difficult standard with one Very Difficult pitch. After reaching the first of the great rocky teeth which form the summit, access to the others is severely hampered by dense heather ($\frac{1}{2}$ hour for 100 yds). Spending one night at the campsite, the expedition can be completed in 2 days.

It is most advisable to employ a guide on Kadam. The paths are rarely used and are often very difficult to follow and much time can be wasted without a guide. Most parties take a few porters, but if a party can dispense with the need for porters it is preferable as the local people are not very satisfactory at this job.

Both guide and porters are best obtained through the Jakait Chief at Moruita and can be arranged in advance through the District Commissioner, Moroto. The best guide, who knows both peaks, is Guido Lowot of Moruita. Guides should be paid about 8/- per day and porters about 4/- to 5/- but this is a matter for negotiation. They should be provided with some sugar and an evening meal.

Maps
1:50,000 Uganda Sheet 45/1.
1:250,000 sheet Kapenguria.
1:100,000 sheet No. 45 prepared by the Geological Survey department and available on enquiry from the Department at Box 9, Entebbe price 5/-.

3. MOROTO MOUNTAIN, 10,118 ft.

This mountain stands alone in the Karamoja district of Uganda and rises some 6,000 ft. above the plains. It is some 400 miles from Nairobi, and could scarcely be tackled in a week-end, but for those with more time to spare it merits a visit and offers beautiful ridge walks.

Approaches:
1. From Kitale via Amudat, to Lokitanyala: then to Katikekile, about 10 miles along the Moroto road.

2. From Mbale, to Moroto along the Watershed Road, then south-east about 20 miles to Katikekile.

About 2 miles west of Katikekile a track leads north to the forest station, 11 miles. This steep track ascends nearly 4,000 ft. and is not suitable for private cars.

Route: From the forest hut, go east and under the first plateau which is separated from the main massif by a narrow ridge. From there an easy path leads up to the western ridge and summit of Sogolomon (9,632 ft.). Time: 1½ to 2 hours. This is beautiful walking in meadow country, with trees and carpets of flowers. Other ridges have more forest and are further away, but would provide several very pleasant days' walking. There are great cliffs on the north side of the mountain. *No water is available.* Permission to pass through Karasuk is required from Kitale, and for the mountain itself from the Forest Department, Moroto.

Maps
1:250,000 Moroto
1:50,000 Uganda Sheet 27/3

4. Turkana and Karasuk

These groups of hills lie in the large area of country bounded by the Turkwel (Tirrikoel) gorge on the south, the Turkwel river on the east and the Amudat-Lodwar road on the west and north, except for Ngithigerr which lies north of the Lodwar road. The hills separate Turkana from Karamoja in Uganda. Turkana is at present administered by Uganda, from which the area is most conveniently approached. The hills rise to 8 or 9 thousand feet. They are dry, sparsely populated and rarely visited. An account of the Turkwel gorge which makes an extremely interesting expedition on the border of this area is also included in this book.

Approaches: All of these hills are approached from the road which runs from Kitale to Moroto and Lodwar. Except for Ngithigerr the hills are reached from tracks which branch off from a long north-south track some miles east of the Kitale-Lodwar Road, which is a continuation of an old K.A.R. Wagon road. This track, which is for Land Rovers only, crosses numerous rivers which can rise very quickly. The track can be got onto conveniently at Amudat (85 miles from Kitale) just north of the Kanyangaren river. The track eventually comes out on the main road at Lokitanyala, near the junction of the road from Moroto to Lodwar. It is open for most of the year. The hills will be described from north to south.

4. MURUA NGITHIGERR, 7,050 ft.

The name means the hill of the Ngithigerr, after a Turkana tribe which used to graze it. First recorded ascent by Capt. the Baron Eric von Otter, K.A.R. in 1921, noted by Lytton.

Approach: From Lodwar by Land Rover and by guesswork over the plains to Lomeyen. 40 miles—5 hours.

Route: From Lomeyen on foot by a stock trail to the Great Glade. Then north through forest on stock trail to Brown's Bath Glade, then by an obvious route onto the main ridge, then visible. The summit is near the northern end of the main east wall, a steep-sided bare grass ridge, with precipices on the eastern face. The summit area is deeply dissected by gorges leading west, so keep to the east. *Water* is available here.

This mountain should only be attempted by well equipped parties, since a mechanical defect could mean a long hot walk out.

Permission required from Lodwar, where guides are obtainable.

Maps
1:250,000 Lodwar
1:100,000 Sheet 34
1:10,000 sketch map by Brown may be seen at the D.C.'s office in Lodwar.

5. CHEMONGERIT HILLS, 6,000 ft. approx.

(From *kerit* meaning leopard and *mong* meaning to come out—where the leopard came out.)

A very prominent group of hills, rising to 6,000 ft. The hills are very wild and rarely visited. They may be approached from Kokidodoka on the lower road, from where a track runs south to the Kakep Pass.

Maps
1:250,000 Moroto

6. KAPITUGEN, 9,000 ft. approx.
   (Home of the Tugen.)

7. KACHAGALAU, 9,156 ft.

8. LOROSUK, 9,000 ft approx.

These fine peaks are best reached by following the track from Amudat to Alale (30 miles). From here a track goes off just before the river to the east towards the hills. From the end of this track (*spring*) the col between Kachagalau and Lorosuk can be reached through the forest in half an hour, whence the summits of either of these mountains can be reached in 2-4 hours. Kapitugen, the northernmost of the three is best approached by continuing along the main track through Alale northward for about five miles when a track going in towards Kapitugen will be seen. Follow this as far as possible and go straight for the summit.

Maps
1:250,000 Moroto
1:50,000 Sheet 50/1

9. TENUS, 8,361 ft.

10. KAPCHOLIO, 9,000 ft. approx.
   (Place of the waterfall or precipice.)

Take the track from Amudat to Alale. About half way between Amudat and Alale a track goes off to the north-east to the Kamila river. From this point either Tenus or Kapcholio can be reached.

Maps
1:250,000, Moroto; Kapenguria
1:50,000 Sheet 50/3

11. TARAKIT, 8,259 ft.

(From *tarakwet*—cedar tree.)
Take the track from Amudat to Kasei village. The final portion of the road requires a Land Rover. Tarakit and Sepich are reached from tracks which leave the Kasei road some miles before the village.

Maps
1:250,000 Moroto
1:50,000 Sheet 50/3

12. KAPCHOK, 6,970 ft.

(From *choket*—karasuk for grain storage house, and *kap*—home of; hence place of grain stores.)

A very prominent hill some 15 miles south of Amudat. It consists of a long ridge with a rock peak at one end. Take the Kitale-Amudat road as far as Kunyao village. From Kunyao village a two hour walk brings one to the base of the mountain. From here the north-west flank of the mountain can be ascended to a saddle. From this point it is 1½ hours to the summit, and scrambling is involved.

Maps
1:250,000 Kapenguria
1:50,000 Sheet 62/1

13. SEPICH, 8,000 ft. approx.

This mountain is reached by the same route as for Tarakit (see no. 11).

TURKWEL GORGE

The gorge is included in this guide, for it is an extremely interesting and little known area within these mountains.

Approach: Turn off right from main Kitale road about 1½ miles south of Kunyao bridge (the only proper bridge after the Suam at Kacheliba) and 16 miles south of Amudat. The track which is 27 miles long goes to Korpu, at the head of the gorge. It is very rough and follows the north (left) bank of the Suam. It thus crosses the Kanyangarong and Kabien rivers as they enter the Suam. Both of these are 30 yards wide, sandy and treacherous and, if they rise, one could be held up for a week. This is therefore a trip for the dry season only. Two vehicles are desirable. Excellent views of the gorge and of the Turkana plain can be obtained by walking over the hills to its south. A descent into the gorge makes an excellent expedition. See H. A. Osmaston, The Turkwel Gorge, in the *Bulletin of the Mountain Club of Uganda* No. 7, 1960/61 for a good account.

Maps
1:250,000 Kapenguria
1:50,000 Sheet 62/2

5. *The Pokot and Cherangani Hills*

These hills lie north of Eldoret and east of Kitale. Their summits which rise to over 10,000 ft., lie at the north end of the spectacular Elgeyo Escarpment. Unlike many of Kenya's hills, the Cheranganis are of crystalline, not of volcanic origin. The hills are mainly forested, though much has been cleared, and there is good grazing land. Some cultivation is found up to 10,000 ft. At the higher altitudes giant heather, lobelia and groundsel occur on the moorlands. At the northern end of the range, north of the Marich pass, lies the Sekerr range.

15. SEKERR, 10,910 ft. (Seger)

First recorded ascent, J. G. Hamilton-Ross, 23/2/1923. Mtelo is the sacred Suk mountain. Suk dead are buried facing it.

Approach: From Kapenguria drive to Akeriemet shop in the Marich pass. 47 miles of twisting and steep road, passable to cars.

Route: From the shop, first wade across the Marun river: then follow a stony path (from a point 200 yards downstream of fording place) up the valley opposite and over first saddle to a water hole among palm trees on the left (2 hours). Continue steeply up to an old road, now impassable to all vehicles, to a ridge above Mbara; descend to Chief's Camp (2½ hours). Camp in or near Mbara. From Mbara proceed westwards on southern flank of valley up a clear path to col in 3 hours. *Water* is available at Mbara, and usually 40 minutes below col. From the col climb up the ridge to top of the forest (1½ hours), then on through heather in 1½ hours to the summit (Mtelo). Descent to roadhead takes 7 hours: Mbara is approximately half way. Guides are usually obtainable at Mbara. Pass necessary from Kitale. There is a fine view from the summit.

Maps
1:250,000 Kapenguria
1:50,000 Sheet 62/4

16. SONDHANG, 10,520 ft.

Approach 1. Kapenguria to Kaibwibich Rest House (20 miles). Continue a further 6 miles and turn off left along a Land Rover track. Follow this to the end (22 miles).

Route 1. Walk north along ridge to reach summit in 6–8 miles. Mainly grassland.

Approach 2. Sigor to Kokwatandwa School (3 hours).

Route 2. Climb to moorland in 2 hours and on to summit in a further hour.

Approach 3. Sebit to Parua by Land Rover.

Route 3. From here a steep walk up mountain track leads to ridge and thence to summit. *Water* near top.

Maps
1:250,000 Kapenguria
1:50,000 Sheet 75/2

17. TAVACH, 10,814 ft.
(*Tabach*—a steep slope.)

Take the Cherangani Highway from Kapenguria and turn off along the Land Rover track to Sondhang. The hill is easily reached from a suitable point along this road.

Maps
1:250,000 Kapenguria
1:50,000 Sheet 75/2

18. KOH, 9,000 ft. approx.

Approach: Two miles south of Sigor a track goes off to the right to Tamkal market.

Route: Before reaching the market a track left affords the most convenient access to the hill, which is a good view point.

Maps
1:250,000 Kapenguria
1:50,000 Sheet 76/1

19. CHEMNIROT, 11,000 ft.

A high top NNE of Kamelogon. Could be approached by the same route as Kamelogon, (see no. 21). Alternatively, approach from Tamkal market and follow up the Marin river. A guide is desirable.

Maps
1:250,000 Kapenguria
1:50,000 Sheet 76/1

20. CHESUGO, 10,100 ft. approx.

Approach: From Chesegon village, 25 miles south of Sigor on Kabarnet road. Start at the chief's compound.

Route: The climb takes 7–8 hours and traverses forest and bamboo. A guide is desirable. *Water* near summit.

Maps
1:250,000 Kapenguria
1:50,000 Sheet 76/1

21. KAMELOGON, 11,540 ft.

Highest point of Cherangani Hills. (*Mologoonik*—a tree found on the mountain which bears fruit.)

Route: From Kailelekelat go north and north-east round the head of the Arror valley. A moorland and forest route with plentiful water. Time: probably 4 hours.

Maps
1:250,000 Kapenguria
1:50,000 Sheet 75/2

22. KALELEKELAT (OR KALELAIGELAT), 10,991 ft.
(Hill of the white teeth, referring to boulders strewn on the hillside).

Approach 1. Take the Cherangani Highway to Kaibwibich Rest House; continue a further six miles and turn off left along the Land Rover track to Sondhang. This track passes within half a mile of the summit to the north. *Water* on spot.

Approach 2. Continue along the Cherangani Highway to Labot Rest House whence a Land Rover track goes to Kabiego.

Route 2. From Kabiego over grassland, skirting Kapsitotwa, to a col below the summit (1½ hours). The area contains much evidence of previous occupation by the Sirikwa peoples.

Route 3. From Kapsoit duka walk 8 miles to the north-east.

Maps
1:250,000 Kapenguria
1:50,000 Sheet 75/4

23. LONGOSWA, 11,000 ft. approx.
(*Lolng'osua* is the Maasai name for the desert date tree, *Balanites Aegyptica*. It is common for Maasai to name mountains after the most common tree or shrub to be found on the hill.)

Approach: Make for Labot P. P. (See Kaisungur). About 2 miles north of Labot is a cross road and duka. Take the track that turns west and leads to the chief's office. Continue as far as the chief's house (10 miles from Labot) and carry on for two more miles to the Arror river. Before crossing this river on the right under some big trees is the D.C.'s camp. Leave vehicle here.

Route: Cross river and walk east on mag. bearing 106° for about two hours. The track then enters thick forest which is traversed for a further two hours to reach summit. *Water* at summit. A guide can be obtained at Kaptalumwa chief's camp or at Tangul D.C.'s camp.

Maps
1:250,000 Kapenguria
1:50,000 Sheet 76/3

24. KIPKUNURR, 10,049 ft.
(*Kunurr*—crooked—the crooked hill.)

A peak on a long ridge west of Marakwet (Kapsowar) village.

Approach: From the Kapenguria-Labot road. Or join this road from Eldoret, via the Moiben-Marakwet-Tambach road. The route starts at an open area shortly before entering forest at the point at which the Moiben river crosses the Labot-Marakwet road, some 10 or 12 miles south-west of Marakwet.

Route: Walk roughly north, crossing two streams with shambas between, then climb up on the ridge. Follow this northward. The trig. point is reached in 2-3 hours, but the ridge to the north is higher.

Maps
1:250,000 Kapenguria
1:50,000 Sheet 76/3

25. KAIPOS, 7,744 ft.
(Pokot—a steep mountain). A westerly spur of the Cheranganis above Kapenguria.

Approach: From Kitale take the eastbound road to Cherangani for 2 miles. Take the left hand road and continue along it for 7 miles until it reaches the road to Hoey's Bridge. Here turn left onto the road to Kapenguria. Continue along this road for one mile and turn right at the road marked Barnley, 7 miles. Follow this road to Barnley's farm. From here enquire for the best route. From the road head to the summit is approximately 2 hours on foot.

Maps
1:250,000 Kapenguria
1:50,000 Sheet 75/3

26. KAIBWIBICH, 8,817 ft.
(Marakwet—where people were swept away.)

Approach: Take the Cherangani Highway from Kapenguria to Kaibwibich Rest House. The summit is approximately 500 yards from the road.

Maps
1:250,000 Kapenguria
1:50,000 Sheet 75/4

27. KAISUNGUR, 10,391 ft.
Take the Cherangani Highway to the highest point reached by the road directly above the D.C.'s Rest Camp and Police Post six miles beyond Kapsoit. The summit is on the west side of the road and may be reached in 20 min.

Maps
1:250,000 Kapenguria
1:50,000 Sheet 75/4

28. CHEMURKOI, 9,547 ft.
   (Marakwet—overhanging rock)

Approach: Proceed along the Cherangani Highway south of Labot P.P. until the hill is seen to the south, some five miles away.

Route: A path leads off from the road at this nearest point, by which the summit can be reached in approximately 2 hours.

Maps
1:250,000 Kapenguria
1:50,000 Sheet 89/2

29. KAPSILIAT, 8,539 ft.
(*Siliat* is a plant commonly found on the mountain—meaning home of this plant.)

Approach: via the Moiben-Karona road which leads to Kapsiliat estate. The road into the estate is just short of the Police Post barrier.

Route: A short 15 minute ascent directly above the estate house.

Maps
1:250,000 Kapenguria
1:50,000 Sheet 89/2

6. Mount Marsabit

30. MOUNT MARSABIT, 5,599 ft.
   (Place of cold.)

An isolated forested mountain in the far north of Kenya. On the summit is a large crater lake—Lake Paradise. The mountain is the main feature of the Marsabit National Park. The mountain rises about 3,000 ft. above the surrounding plains. A motorable track goes from the boma to about 5,000 ft.

Approach: The mountain is very remote—about 150 miles due north of the Uaso Nyiro river. It is reached by a road from Isiolo and Archer's Post. It is necessary to take reserve water and petrol and a minimum of two cars is needed to make the journey from Archer's Post. There is a log cabin Safari Lodge at Marsabit. The cabin has accommodation for four people and has basic furniture. Before visiting the area it is essential to contact the Provincial Commissioner, Isiolo.

Maps
1:250,000 Marsabit

7. The Mountains of Samburu

The massifs and ranges of Samburu lie in the vast area of largely arid country inhabited by pastoral tribes, which lies between Maralal and the Ethiopian border, and which formerly formed part of the Northern Frontier District. The country is remote and the mountains are dramatic, often forest covered, and game abounds on them. Closed district permits are required for expeditions into this area. Land Rovers are desirable. At the time of writing, this fascinating area cannot be visited, except for the area around Maralal, on account of shifta activity in the north. Many early European travellers passed through this country, including Donaldson Smith, Delamere, Teleki and von Höhnel.

31. KULAL, 7,522 ft.
(Meeting place for the elders).

Kulal is a volcano of Tertiary age, later violently split, and heavily eroded. The two summits are joined by a knife-edged ridge, as yet uncrossed, and probably very difficult. Arabal, the higher summit, is on the north side, and Ladarabach to the south. Both are forested. First recorded ascent by P. Maud, 1903.

Approach: By Land Rover only, north from Maralal via Baragoi and South Horr in 7–8 hours.

Route: The ascent consists of an easy walk to either summit in 5–6 hours. Forest Guards are available to act as guides in the forest.

Permission from Maralal is required to use the forest huts which exist on both sides of Kulal.

Maps
1:250,000 South Horr
1:100,000 Sheet 41

32. NYIRU, 9,283 ft.
(Oldoinyo Ng'iro—the brown mountain. It is composed mainly of pinkish granite).

Approach: From Maralal, via Baragoi and Kowop; then left for Tum, or right for South Horr. About 5 hours from Maralal (by Land Rover only after Baragoi).

Route 1. From Tum Forest Camp, up to grass glade in 2 hours, then either northwest to the top in $2\frac{1}{2}$ hours, or to Kuskuss summit at the head of the Horr river. The NW summit has the finer view.

Route 2. From South Horr proceed to Logok glade by stock trails; then out of the glade, and on to the crest, and the summit. Time: 5–6 hours from start.

Either summit can be reached in a day from Tum, or the massif can be traversed in a hard day, without crossing either summit. The top of the mountain is a largely forested area, of several square miles, made up of many ridges and glades, and well worth a few days' visit. At the end of a grassy ridge, at the N.W. end of the massif is a trig. point, affording views over Lake Rudolf. There are many rocky outcrops, especially on the Tum side. Permission is required from Maralal. Guides —honey hunters—are available from Tum or South Horr. Donkeys can be hired at 21 days' notice, through Maralal. The cost is 3/- per day, plus syce 2/- per day. The donkeys carry a maximum load of 80 lbs. It is desirable not to use the local method of harnessing, but instead to pack in bags.

Maps
1:250,000 South Horr
1:100,000 Sheet 53

NDOTO RANGE

33. OLDOINYO NDOTO (BOKKOL), 8,313 ft.
(Maasai—Oldoinyo Loontoto—mountain of small rocks.)

This is the N. W. end of the Ndoto Range. The summit is a bare dome of grass and helychrysum. Steep rocky slopes to the west and north.

Approach: Maralal to Baragoi (3 hours). Continue for 1 hour to Lesirikon.
The road from Baragoi is not recommended for saloon cars.

Route: Follow the right hand side of valley from Lesirikon spring, under a bosa to a saddle between fore ridge and main mass. Cross this and contour on to $\frac{1}{2}$ stock trail for a $\frac{1}{2}$ mile then follow trail up the side of dome. Time: 5 hours up, 3 down. *Water* can be had at Nderobo wells on the back of first ridge above Lesirikon, and in small glades on the side of the dome. Guides could be provided at 21 days' notice through local officials.

Maps
1:250,000 Maralal
1:100,000 Sheet 66

34. ALIMISION, 8,650 ft.
The highest point of the Ndoto Range, forming a knife edge ridge of grass and crags.

Approach: From Baragoi to Lesirikon and on to Arsim (5 hours). Branch off to Arsim 5 miles short of Illaut.

Route 1. From the Forest Guard post at Arsim take a cattle track to Suruan (1 day). From Suruan climb along the crest to summit and return to Suruan in 1 day.

Route 2. From Lesirikon cross Taugat Pass below Ambar River to Ntassate Ridge (5 hours). Take a stock trail on to Suruan Mountain (4 hours). Proceed by saddles to summit in a further 3 hours. 2 days needed for trip. A Rest House is planned at Suruan.

Maps
1:250,000 Maralal
1:100,000 Sheet 66

MATHEWS RANGE

The Mathews range was named by Count Teleki after General (later Sir) Lloyd Mathews, the one-time Commander-in-Chief of the army of the Sultan of Zanzibar, and later First Secretary to the Zanzibar Government. The range is remote and rarely visited. Access is difficult. Land Rover only.

35. OLDOINYO LENGEYO, 7,505 ft.
(Oldoinyo Lekiyio—mountain of the child.)

The most northerly summit in the Mathews range.

Approach: Drive from Archer's Post to Lodosoit (3 hours). Continue to Gihura (3 hours) by Land Rover only.

Route: From Gihura walk up to the saddle between Il Bission and the main range, and follow a game track to the summit. Game is abundant.

Maps
1:250,000 Maralal
1:100,000 Sheet 79

36. MATHEWS PEAK, 7,792 ft.

Approach: Take the road from Archer's Post to Marsabit. About 45 miles from Archer's Post a track (Land Rover only) goes off W and NW to Lodosoit trading centre. From there a track crosses the river and continues NW. After 3 miles there is a left fork. Continue along the left fork, as for Lengeyo, but branch off at the point at which the track gets nearest to the peak. From here tracks may be found which can be used to approach nearer the mountain.

Route: Traverse thick bush until the north-east slopes of the mountain are reached. Enter the forest on game trails and make for the summit. Game is abundant. Compass useful. From the plains the summit is a stiff ascent of 4,000 ft. Time: 6 hours.

Maps
1:250,000 Laisamis and Maralal
1:100,000 Sheet 79

37. MATHEWS SOUTH PEAK, 7,497 ft.

Approach: Approach from the Wamba-Barsaloi road. Some 3 miles east of the zero meridian a track branches off north to Il Mara Muroi. Follow this track some 8 miles to a point where five tracks meet. From here a track continues east to near the forest edge.

Route: Enter the forest on game trails and follow to the summit which lies at the eastern end of the hill.

Maps
1:250,000 Maralal
1:100,000 Sheet 79

*   *   *

38. WARGES, 8,820 ft.
(Wamba Mountain)

Approach: From Isiolo, via Archer's Post, to Wamba (2 hours). Or from Thomson's Falls, via Maralal to Wamba (4 hours). Passable for cars.

Route 1. From Wamba, walk or drive (Land Rover) for 1½ miles on right bank of stream. Continue on foot up valley, and out onto ridges to the south where the valley bends towards the main massif. Go up a ridge, over a subsidiary summit and continue steeply to the top. A trig. point in a small clearing marks the summit, reached in 5-6 hours. Extensive views.

Route 2. Leave Wamba on the Isiolo road (bad gullies) and proceed for about six miles. On rounding a spur on the left of the road, a track goes off to the left. Follow this for about ¾ mile to the foot of a valley north of Koitong village. From here the path to the summit, which eventually joins the first route, takes about 4½-5 hours. Elephant are often found in the valley, and their trails may provide the easiest route up. If guides are required, arrange well in advance through Wamba. *Water* ½ mile west (20 minutes).

Maps
1:250,000 Rumuruti.
1:50,000 Sheet 93/2

39. OLOLOKWE, 6,080 ft.
(Oldoinyo Sabachi)
Ololokwe, though lower than 7,000 ft., is included in view of its interest and prominence.

Approach: From Isiolo, via Archer's Post. Proceed along the Marsabit road past the Great Wall of the mountain, till a valley appears on the north side. Drive up this for ½ mile, to the roadhead. This is 2 hours from Isiolo.

Route: Climb up the spur, through bush, at the north end of the Great Wall, to a rocky knob—1½ hours: then follow a rhino trail to bare rocks, and along the rim to the Breakfast Tree, the only tree on the summit. The mountain has no identifiable summit, but the tree, visible from below, is probably near it. There are stock trails from the head of the valley mentioned, and up the western side of the mountain. The main attraction of the ascent is the walk for several miles along the top of the crags which are up to 1,300 ft. high. There are many rhino on the mountain.

Maps
1:250,000 Garba Tula
1:50,000 Sabachi—Sheet 94/4

40. LOSIOLO, 8,104 ft.
(Samburu name for species of tree)
Approach: Take the Baragoi road for about 16 miles from Maralal. At the summit of the escarpment, opposite a farm and pine plantation to the right (opposite the Poror track), a motorable track goes off to the left. Follow this track for 6 miles to

the edge of the escarpment where the vehicle must be left. Losiolo is visible for most of the way.

Route: Walk a short distance south and descend by a well marked track into the forested gorge to a forest path. Follow this for about a mile across another gorge to reach the summit which is a projection into the valley. Losiolo is one of the finest view points in Kenya.

Maps
1:250,000 Maralal
1:50,000 Sheet 78/3

41. POROR, 8,473 ft.
(Maasai—*olporrorr*—age set.)
The highest point of an almost bare dome-shaped hill north of Maralal.

Approach: Take the Baragoi road for about 16 miles. On the right (see 40, Losiolo), there is a track leading to the hill-top in a few minutes.

Maps
1:250,000 Maralal
1:50,000 Sheet 78/3

42. PAUA, 7,396 ft.
A summit some six miles south east of Maralal, perhaps 1,000 ft. above the general elevation of the country. Approached by forest roads.

Maps
1:250,000 Maralal
1:50,000 Sheet 78/3

43. LESHINGEITA, 7,237 ft.
(Samburu for fish spawn—a possible reference to the appearance of the hill.)
Approach: From Wamba take the Baragoi road for about 56 miles until the Baragoi river is reached. About two miles back towards Wamba the track goes off leading to Leshingeita. It is possible to take a Land Rover along this track to the Samburu settlements around the foot of the mountain.

Route: Strike up the north-east slopes to the summit ridge. The highest point is marked by a cairn. Nearest *water* is in Oporoi river, if you dig.

Maps
1:250,000 Maralal
1:50,000 Sheet 78/4

8. The Tuken or Kamasia Hills

The Tuken or Kamasia hills stretch roughly northwards from the eastern end of the Lembus forest for some 60 miles and are then separated from the Tiati outlier by the Kito pass between Kolloa and Nginyang. The summits run from about 9,000 ft. in the south to about 6,000 ft. in the north. The range separates the Kerio valley from the main floor of the Rift Valley. The hills offer a number of excellent easy excursions which afford magnificent views of the Cheranganis, the Elgeyo escarpment, the lower Rift, Baringo and the Laikipia escarpment. Originally densely forested on the higher levels, most land with agricultural potential has now been cleared. Some fine stands of natural forest remain in the gazetted forest areas. There are many campsites with water. Guides are readily available if required.

Approach: The main roads to Kabarnet, either from Nakuru via Mogotio and Marigat, or from Eldoret via Tambach and Cheblock Bridge are easily passable for saloon cars, except in heavy rains. The road from Eldama Ravine to Tenges, Kabarnet, and northwards, is much more difficult, with many dongas and steep gradients but it is practicable for saloon cars and is scenically well worth the effort. There are many other roads or jeep tracks to the better known viewpoints. From these access tracks even the least accessible summits are seldom more than 1½ hours, but a walk up the hills from either of the valleys may mean a 5 or 6 hour trip. Permission necessary from D. O. Eldama Ravine (tel. 6), or D. C. Kabarnet (Radiocall Nairobi 2825). Access is difficult during rains.

51. TIATI, 7,713 ft.
    (Tuken—*tiat*—strong, thick or heavy—a reference to the massive base of the mountain.)

A northerly outlier which lies some 15 miles east of the Kerio river. The summit is a prominent rocky knob rising out of the forest. Magnificent views.

Approach: Either down the Kerio valley from Tambach, or from Kabarnet, or from Kapenguria via the Marich pass to Tot trading centre. These routes are extremely slow. From Tot a track leads off eastwards and crosses the Kerio river by suspension bridge in about four miles. Follow this track to Kolloa (12 miles from Tot). At Kolloa guides may be obtained.

Route: From Kolloa walk for four hours across waterless country to Kabowan at the foot of the mountain. Kabowan is in line with the peak from Kolloa (camp). *Water* can sometimes be found by digging in the sand of the river bed below the rocks of the dry waterfall. From Kabowan the climb to the peak takes about 2¼ hours. There is *no water* en route. The climb is continuous and easy along a footpath which for much of the way traverses a very steep hillside. Guides available from Kolloa if required but they are unlikely to speak Swahili.

Kilimanjaro sugarbush (*Protea Kilimandscharica*)

Yellow everlasting flowers
(*Helichrysum setosum*)

Giant heath (*Erica arborea*) and Nandi everlasting flowers (*Helichrysum nondense*) on
Mount Kenya

52. SAIMO (Ketingwan), 8,207 ft.
(Tuken—steep, or precipice).

Saimo is the highest point of a large hill in a range running south-north into the centre of the Rift Valley. The summit is the centre of three peaks.

Approach: Start from Kabarnet. Take the road to Kabartonjo (13 miles). At the far end of Kabartonjo dukas take a bush track sharp left (Land Rover only) which leads to Bartolimo after 9 very slow miles.

Route: Follow footpath through shambas up side of hill direct to summit. Time: 1½ hours. The ascent is also possible from Kampi ya Samaki for the very fit.

Maps
1:250,000 Eldoret
1:50,000 Sheet 90/4

53. MAROP, 7567 ft.
(Place of rain.)

A prominent conical hill lying just to the north of the Kabarnet to Marigat road.

Approach: From Kabarnet take the Marigat road for about 7 miles past Kituro RC mission to Kituro market. At Kituro market Marop can be seen about 2-3 miles away on a bearing of 27°.

Route: Take a path past the most easterly duka to arap Kimngetuny's house. The path turns east and crosses a small dry valley on to Tarambas ridge. It follows the western edge of Tarambas ridge up to the end and it continues on the top of another smaller ridge up to the foot of Marop hill. A steep final climb. Time: 1 hour 20 minutes. *No water* near summit.

Maps
1:250,000 Eldoret
1:50,000 Sheet 90/4 and 104/2

54. KIBIMCHOR, 7,699 ft.
(Place of much food—*njoe* is an attic store house.)

Approach: Start 2 miles south of Tenges where, at the highest point of the road, a track goes off west to a quarry, opposite a forestry house.

Route: A track climbs steeply up through shambas and follows the northern end of the mountain round to the west side, where a track contours south through a forested valley to the valley head. Climb up through more shambas and bear east to reach a col south of a forested hump. Follow the ridge south to the summit. An exhilarating ridge walk with fine views. Time: about 1-1½ hours from roadhead. *No water* near summit.

Maps
1:250,000 Eldoret
1:50,000 Sheet 104/2

55. KAPKUT, 9,185 ft.
(Kut is the name given to a clumpy grass—the place where this is found.)

Approach: From Eldama Ravine take the old Sclaters road which runs west to Timboroa. In about 1½ miles a cross road is reached. Turn right here and follow the road which runs in a roughly northerly direction. In about two miles the Lelgel river is crossed at a pleasant grassy clearing near an old saw mill site. At the left fork to Simonia keep straight on for several miles until the road descends very steeply into the gorge of the Perkerra. Continue beyond the river for about a mile and a half through the thick forest along the road to Sigora. On the left of the road a track starts towards Gaisamu. Leave the vehicle here.

Route: The track which is well defined follows a north-westerly line through the forest until the south-eastern flanks of the mountains are reached. From here the track turns north-east and ascends through the forest until the cleared summit of *Gaisamu* is reached (1½ hours). From here a pleasant walk over undulating downland, largely cleared and grazed, but with pleasant stands of forest, takes one in a further 1½ hours to Kapkut.

Alternative Routes

Alternative approaches which may be employed for Kapkut are: 1. From Tenges to Cheplambus (2½ hours). From here the summit may be reached in five hours. 2. From Eldama Ravine to Sirwa (2 hours). Camp. Time: 4 hours to summit.

Maps
1:250,000 Eldoret
1:50,000 104/3

56. GAISAMU, 8,943 ft.
Approach and Route: See Kapkut (No. 55)

OTHER FEATURES OF INTEREST

Lake Baringo can be reached via Marigat and Kampi ya Samaki in good saloon cars. Good camp sites. Fish Eagle Safari Camp is located here. Good fishing. Many mosquitoes. Crocodiles docile.

Lake Hannington can be reached via Maji ya Moto (good camp site, and bathing in hot springs). From here a track (Land Rover only) goes to the lake where flamingos, steam jets and geysers can be seen. Alternatively the lake can be reached on foot from the camp site in 2½ hours.

Maps
1:250,000 Kisumu Nakuru
1:250,000 Eldoret
1:250,000 Rumuruti (for Lakes Baringo and Hannington).
1:50,000 Sheet 104/2.

9. *The Aberdare Range*

The Aberdare range was named in 1884, by J. J. Thomson after Lord Aberdare, then the President of the Royal Geographical Society. The range, which is of volcanic origin, lies almost directly north of Nairobi. It maintains a height of over 9,000 ft. for a distance of over 40 miles, and divides Kikuyuland on the east from the Rift Valley on the west. The western face, overlooking the Kinangop plateau and the Rift Valley below it, is very steep whereas the eastern slopes descend more gently from the moorlands, through the forest belt, to the Kikuyu cultivated lands below 7,000 ft. Rain is plentiful on the east side and there are many rivers, most of which have cut deep valleys as in the head-streams of the Ewaso Ngiro, the Tana and the Thika. Frost is common above 9,000 ft. There are three principal summits in the range and one outlier, Kipipiri.

The peaks are accessible through North or South Kinangop, Thomson's Falls, Nyeri, Fort Hall, Thika or from the Aberdares National Parks road. Permission is required from Warden of Mountain National Parks, Nyeri, for the main peaks of the Aberdares, and from the Forest Department, N. Kinangop, for Kipipiri.

61. KIPIPIRI, 10,987 ft.

> (Maasai—*ilkipirin*—an instrument used to stir when cooking.)

This is a single flat topped dome, standing apart from, and west of, the main massif.

62. OLDOINYO LA SATIMA, 13,120 ft.

> (Maasai—mountain of the young bull.)

This is the northernmost summit, the highest swelling of a horseshoe ridge enclosing the headwaters of the Amboni river, marked by a theodolite pedestal and some wooden beacons. A rocky knob to the north looks higher.

63. THE KINANGOP, 12,816 ft.

> (*Ilkinopop* in Maasai—"the owners of the land". The area originally belonged to the Laikipiak Maasai but was taken and so named by the Purko when they defeated the Laikipiak about 1875 and dispersed them. The area is called *Nyandarua* in Kikuyu.)

This is a much more impressive peak than Satima. It lies twenty miles to the south of Satima, from which it is divided by a lower area, some of it swampy. The northernmost of its three rock bosses is the highest.

64. THE ELEPHANT, 11,780 ft.

> (A reference to the obvious elephant-like outline of the ridge when seen from South Kinangop.)

This is the long ridge to south. There is no clear feature to mark the summit, which is towards the northern end.

KIPIPIRI

Approach: From Nairobi to the N. Kinangop entry to National Parks road in 2½ hours. Turn left to Geta, just before this gate, and continue for 2 miles.

Route: Climb steeply up a 30 ft. wide firebreak on right to summit where route finding is difficult. Alternative routes from Wanjohi valley on north, or from Kipipiri road to west.

SATIMA

1. From Nyeri

Approach: Take the road to Mweiga. Continue along the Rumuruti road, crossing a small bridge over the Amboni stream. One mile from Mweiga turn left at Kieni West Harambee school. At mile 6 turn left at Naro-Moru-Thomson's Falls Road. At mile 8 fork left to Pura Milk Factory. At the factory turn left on to Wandare's track. In 300 yards this turns right and passes between fences to reach a forest gate at mile 11. Continue and at mile 15 fork right. The end of the track is reached at mile 17, where there is a hut. (Advance permission to use the road must be obtained from National Parks and Forestry Department.) A dry weather route, for Land Rover only.

Route: From the end of the road walk a mile through the forest due west. On leaving the forest walk due NW about three miles on NE slope of ridge which runs SE—NW. Tributaries of Uaso Nyiro visible on right. Country here is open and grassy. Try to follow a buffalo trail if possible as the terrain is otherwise difficult to traverse. Aim for a point about ¼ mile east of point 12548. After reaching this point turn left to nearest ridge and follow in NW direction. After 2 miles the ridge turns SW to the highest point of Satima. Time: 4 hours.

2. From Thomson's Falls

Approach: From Thomson's Falls follow the Nanyuki road for about four miles, then turn right at Ndaragwa road. At mile 12 is the Ndaragwa turning. Keep straight on past this. At mile 25 is a village. Enquire here for Forest Department Gate (permit necessary). From the village, the track which is motorable by cars in dry weather is followed to mile 31, roughly between a prominent rock stack on the right, known as the First Twin, and Eland Hill (fire tower) on the left. There is a good camp site on the left of the road.

Route: Directly opposite the campsite a track goes off from the First Twin, past the Second Twin. Follow this and strike off it to Muirs Massif. In front will be seen an extensive basin with large volcanic outcrops on the west. Cross the basin over fairly hard going, and climb up over moorland to reach the summit. Time: 3-4 hours from campsite. *No water.*

3. From Queen's Gate

Approach: Drive to summit of National Parks road, via North Kinangop.
Route: From a point 200 yards west of the road summit a large game trail leads off north. The walk is said to take 6 hours. A guide is probably desirable.

KINANGOP *and*
THE ELEPHANT

The first recorded ascent of Kinangop was made in 1907 by a party led by Father Fillipe Perlo from the mission at Tusa. A shrine and cross were erected on the summit and mass was celebrated.

1. From South Kinangop

Approach: From Njabini Forest Station proceed, preferably by Land Rover, for about 3 miles along the Fort Hall track.

Route: Left up a cut line through bamboo, then steeply up ridge to hut at south end of The Elephant, in 3 hours. Continue to the summit of The Elephant, then down a steep valley to east (right), to col, then up ridge; pass east (for the best view) of the first two rock pinnacles. Scramble up the third, which is the Kinangop, by north or south ridges, or up vegetable covered ledges on west. This is an airy summit, in a generally moorland area, reached in about 3 hours from The Elephant. It is possible to descend to North Kinangop via Mai Mahoro forest station in 5 hours. Alternatively, descend by the Tuso track, an old Maasai route from the Rift to Nyeri. This is a very long route.

2. From Fort Hall

Approach: Drive west to Kanyenyeini, and then on to the forest edge 4 miles above Karuri.

Route: Follow game trails along ridge between Maragua and North Mathioya rivers. This may take all day.

3. From Thika

Approach: Drive to Mairi, 30 miles, and forest station beyond. Turn right (Land Rover only) where road to S. Kinangop veers left, then up steep hill and on to end of track, 3 miles.

Route: Follow well used track through forest, to join cut line route through bamboo, after crossing crest of ridge. 1½–2 hours. Then follow South Kinangop route to The Elephant. Time: 2–3 hours.

Other Routes: The Kinangop may also be approached from North Kinangop, by Land Rover to the Isanya fire tower; then walk up the Tuso track. It could also be reached from the National Park road. There are probably many interesting climbs to be done on the rocky crags near the Satima camp site, and near Kinangop Peak. The moorland vegetation is largely tufted grass, which is exhausting to traverse. Great care is necessary for route finding when mist occurs.

An interesting walk, requiring a minimum of 3 days, and considerable planning, would be a traverse of all the main Aberdare summits.

Maps
1:250,000 Nyeri. This covers the whole range.
1:50,000 Sheet 120/3 for Satima and Kipipiri.
1:50,000 Sheet 143/1 for the Kinangop and The Elephant.

10. Mau

A group of summits on the Mau escarpment which forms part of the western wall of the Great Rift Valley. Much of the Mau is heavily wooded.

65. TINDERET, 8,663 ft.

(From the Kalenjin word *tindir* meaning excessive noise or thunder. Kipsigis have a fable or superstition attributing to Tinderet the origin of each rainy season. Lightning over the mountain means that the rainy season is starting.)

Approach: Near Mtetei on the Equator-Songhor road take a road which runs SE eventually to run along the west bank of the Kasabe River. In 2 miles fork right and follow a track to its farthest south point. Where the track turns east and north there is a big cleared area under tea. It may be possible to drive through the tea estate south to the forest boundary. Leave vehicle here.

Route: Enter the dense rain forest along a track and follow more or less due south approximately along watershed. If the track is located and clear, $1\frac{1}{4}$ hours to summit. Otherwise much longer. Visibility restricted to 10 yards or less. Vegetation, thick forest and bamboo. Summit marked by trig. point. *Water* $\frac{1}{2}$ hour west of summit.

Maps
1:250,000 Kisumu—Nakuru
1:50,000 Sheet 117/2

66. LOLDIAN, 9,878 ft.

(Swahili rendering of the Maasai *Oldoinyo Loltiyani* meaning mountain of bamboos.)

Approach: From Mau Summit take the Eldoret Road across the railway ($\frac{1}{2}$ mile from road junction). After about 2 miles this road meets the main Eldoret-Nakuru road at right angles. Cross over the main road onto a minor farm road opposite. After about a further 2 miles turn right onto a road into Haswell's farm. This continues through the farm directly to the Police and Post Office radio stations' on the top of the hill. The final ascent is very steep and rough but motorable. The highest point of the hill is in thick bamboo forest.

Maps
1:250,000 Kisumu—Nakuru
1:50,000 Sheet 118/1

67. MAU, 10,000 ft.

(Maasai—*mao* a division—e.g. a watershed.)

Approach: From Njoro take the road to the Nessuiet Forest Station. From the forest station follow the road to the Newby sawmill (about 2 miles) and then follow the saw mill forest track to the foot of the hill. The distance from the saw-mill to the foot of the hill is about 7 miles.

Route: Follow the path to the Maasai reserve (Kiblugluge) for about 40 minutes and then turn sharp right and climb along the ridge (very steep on the left side) until the summit (trig. point) is reached.

Maps
1:250,000 Kisumu—Nakuru
1:50,000 Sheet 118/4

68. EBURU, 9,365 ft.
(Maasai—*epuru*—meaning sound of a steam jet.) Partly ascended by J. J. Thomson in 1883.

Approach: From Nairobi to Eburu by Naivasha North Lake road (2 hours).

Route: From Eburu Settlement Scheme under Pt. 8753 follow Rift Valley wall up past a small crater lake and into the forest. A short descent is followed by a nettle filled glade. Then continue up steeply through forest without undergrowth to the summit. The summit is a crescent shaped ridge covered with forest and bamboo. The highest point is not marked.

Maps
1:250,000 Nyeri
1:50,000 Sheet 133/2

69. MELILI, 10,165 ft.
(Maasai—*ilmelili*—the slopes)

1. From Nakuru
Approach: Proceed to Njoro. Turn sharp left at D.C.'s office and proceed 24 miles to Mau Narok. Continue for $3\frac{1}{2}$ miles and just before the crest of a very steep hill turn left at signpost—Powys-Cobb. Proceed through the farm to a locked gate at the old Mau Narok Police Post, where the key for the gate may be obtained. Continue through the forest for three miles and on leaving the forest a Maasai manyatta is seen on the left. From here a track (dry weather only) leaves the road in an easterly direction and approaches the hill.

Route: From the end of the track a 20 minute walk first east then north brings one to the summit.

2. From Naivasha
Approach: From Naivasha South Lake Police Station take the Maiella road. Turn right at the Maiella signboard and follow a Land Rover track to Saakutiek.

Route: Walk from Saakutiek across the valley and straight up the slopes in 2-3 hours. The summit lies SSW of Crater Lake, Naivasha and is the highest point on the Mau escarpment.

Maps
1:250,000 Nyeri
1:50,000 Sheet 133/3

11. *The Mountains of Maasailand*

This section groups the mountains in the area known as Maasailand. Most of the mountains are isolated peaks of volcanic origin and lie in or adjacent to the Great Rift Valley south of the Nairobi-Nakuru road.

71. LONGONOT, 9,111 ft.

(Maasai—oloonong'ot—meaning mountain of the many spurs or steep ridges.)

A prominent volcano in the Rift Valley about 45 miles from Nairobi. The ascent is easily undertaken in a day trip from Nairobi. The first recorded ascent to the crater rim was made by J. J. Thomson in 1883. The first recorded ascent to the summit was made by J. W. Gregory in 1893.

Approach: Take the Nakuru road as far as Longonot level crossing (41 miles).

Turn left down the track immediately before level crossing and follow this to the base of the mountain (4 miles). A gully, one mile short of the trackhead, may be impassable. Cars left unattended at the gully or trackhead are often broken into.

Route: A well defined track on the left bank of the gully leads in about 45 minutes to the crater rim. For the shortest route to the summit follow the crater rim anti-clockwise. The circuit of the crater takes 2½ to 3 hours. There are steam jets inside the crater which can be reached by a steep descent from the north side of the rim.

The circuit affords fine views of the Rift, the Aberdares, the Mau and Lake Naivasha.

Maps
1:250,000 Nyeri
1:50,000 Sheet 133/4

72. SUSWA, 7,732 ft.

(Maasai—place of the dusty plain; the Maasai refer to the summit itself as Oldoinyo Onyokie—the Red Mountain. In Dorobo, *susua* means grass—a reference to the good grazing in the outer crater.)

A prominent volcano 15 miles west of the escarpment on the Nakuru road. The breached crater is 7 miles in diameter and the summit lies at the south side. There is an interesting inner core surrounded by a deep trench. The name is a Maasai term for the whole area. The summit itself is called Oldoinyo Onyokie, the Red Mountain. The first mention of an ascent of Oldoinyo Nyukie is by J. W. Gregory but it seems likely that he was referring to Mount Magaret. There are many interesting lava caves around the flanks of the mountain. Particulars may be had from the Nairobi Caving Group, c/o National Museum, Nairobi. The mountain appears to have been ascended in October 1897 by F. H. Hall, with Blackett and Welby, on the Uganda Railway Survey.

Approach 1. About 36 miles from Nairobi on the road to Naivasha turn left at crossroads signposted Narok. Eight miles after leaving the tarmac turn left at a borehole. Follow a track for five miles in the direction of the base of the mountain. Then turn right along what was the original road to Narok. Follow this for a mile or so and then turn sharp left up a steep indistinct track. This track climbs over lava flows to a manyatta at the plateau. If going to the caves, fork left just beyond the manyatta. A good camp site will be found at the end of the track, about two miles from the manyatta. If the summit is the objective, fork right through a breach into the outer crater and follow the track or pick a convenient route in a south westerly direction to any convenient camp site near the rim of the inner crater. *No water*. This route is for EPCs only. Land Rovers to be preferred. Permission required from D. C. Kajiado and from Akira Ranch, Box 16, Naivasha.

Route 1. The route to the summit follows the west and south sides of the inner crater and takes about 2-2½ hours. There is abundant game on the slopes and in the inner crater.

Approach 2. Take the Narok road as above and proceed for 20 miles until the hill appears to be left behind on the left hand side of the road, where the transmission lines cross the road turn left across open flat grassland. Keep Maasai manyattas on your left and drive as near as possible to the ridge of the crater.

Route 2. From the base of the mountain follow Maasai tracks to the summit. Time: 3-3½ hours.

Approach 3. It is also possible to reach the mountain by descending the escarpment at Ndeiya, near Dagoretti, but this is a more difficult approach. It joins the first approach along the old road to Narok.

Maps
1:250,000 Nairobi
1:50,000 Sheet 147/2

73. LAMWIA, 8,074 ft.

Lamwia is the highest and southernmost of the four distinct peaks of the Ngong Hills which lie prominently on the edge of the Rift Valley some 15 miles southwest of Nairobi. A traverse of the Ngong skyline track is a popular expedition with Nairobi residents and affords fine views. Lamwia, the highest summit, is a corruption of the Maasai word *Ilemuya* which is another name for the Enkidong'i or Oloiboin (ritual expert) clan. The common Maasai name for the hills is Oloo-Laiserr, a name for the descent group to which the Oloiboni's clan belongs. The hills figure importantly in Maasai myths concerning how they originally acquired the first ritual expert or Oloibani family.

There are three legends associated with the Ngong Hills and their symmetrical appearance.

1. When God had finished shaping the world he found that he had dirt between his fingers. He wiped this off upon the earth leaving the shape of the Ngong Hills.

2. A giant who was running across Africa tripped over Mount Kilimanjaro and in trying to save himself from falling crushed the earth to the shape of the Ngong Hills with one hand.

3. An enormous giant terrorised the land occupied by the Maasai, consuming vast numbers of their cattle for his normal sustenance. In desperation the Maasai approached various wild animals for help, asking in turn the lion, the buffalo, the elephant and rhinoceros if they would rid them of this giant. Each of these animals was unable to help, but finally, when they approached the ant, help was obtained. Whilst the giant was sleeping all the ants in that part of Africa carried small particles of earth and buried the giant leaving only the knuckles of one hand above ground and these have since become the Ngong Hills.

Tracks skirt the base of the Ngongs to the east and west and afford an interesting dry weather circular car tour. Along the track to the east there is a memorial to Dennis Finch-Hatton, a close friend of Karen Blixen, the authoress of *Out of Africa*, after whom Karen village was named.

Approaches
1. From the north
Follow a steep signposted track which leaves the road close beside Ngong Police Station. Cars may be driven up to the road barrier below the wireless station on the ridge.

Route: Follow the well defined track along the skyline to the triangulation point on the southernmost summit. Time from wireless station to Lamwia: about 1 hour.

2. From the south

Leave Nairobi by the Magadi road. At mile 15, about three miles beyond Kiserian mission a track goes off to the right up the shoulder of the mountain. It can be followed by saloon cars for about a mile and by Land Rovers to fairly near the summit.

Route: Follow the track which winds to the summit. Time: 1½ hours. Game is often abundant on this side.

Maps
1:250,000 Nairobi
1:50,000 Sheet 148/3

74. LOITA (Subugo), 8,802 ft.
(Loitai is a Maasai tribal name; Subugo is derived from the Maasai *osupuko* meaning dry bush area in which a certain shrub *Dombeya Burgessiae* is dominant.)

Approach: From Narok take the road for Loliondo. After 40 miles Narosura is reached. Continue south from Narosura on the Loliondo road which climbs the escarpment. On top of the Loita escarpment at approx. 50 miles from Narok turn right off the road and climb a very steep grassy slope on to the main Subugo ridge. Proceed along the summit of this ridge to the mountain which is reached about 4 miles from the road. A Land Rover can reach the summit. *Water* in holes *en route.* O. Neuman ascended to the Loita mountains from south of Sosian in 1894.

Maps
1:250,000 Narok
1:50,000 Sheet 159/2

75. SHOMBOLE, 5,132 ft.
(Maasai—*shompole*, meaning place to go slow.)

An old volcano south of Lake Magadi. Very steep ridges with abundant thorny vegetation lead up from all sides to the extensive summit plateau. First recorded ascent in 1904 by G. E. Smith of the Anglo-German Boundary Commission Survey, to 4,850 ft.

Approach: Drive to Magadi ($2\frac{1}{2}$ hours from Nairobi). Continue south through the town and along a track which passes Bird Rock, runs along the lake bed and later skirts the east and south of a swamp to reach a small village at the NW foot of the mountain, 20 miles and $1\frac{1}{2}$ hours SW of Magadi. Continue south past the village (Alangarna), and along the left bank of the Ewaso Ngiro river (Brown river), until the main peaks are nearly due south. Camp sites. Land Rover advised.

Route: Looking south, two obvious peaks can be seen. Make for westerly of the two, along a rocky ridge which in places is very narrow. When this peak is reached the true summit will be seen about $\frac{1}{2}$ mile away. The top of the mountain is covered with dense scrub and bush. The ascent is about 2,500 ft. *Water* in Ewaso Ngiro river, north-west of hill. This is a stiff climb which will take 3–4 hours. Usually very hot. Mosquitoes are abundant. Start very early in the morning if you wish to reach the summit and return to Nairobi on the same day. Pangas essential.

Maps
1:250,000 Nairobi
1:250,000 Amboseli
1:50,000 Sheet 171/1

76. LEMILEBLU, 7,050 ft.
(Maasai—*ilemelepo*—dry hills)

Approach: Take the Namanga road from Nairobi. About 60 miles from Nairobi. just after an S bend, a broad cattle track leads off right to the foot of the hills half a mile away. Leave vehicle here, or on main road.

Route: Cross the first low ridge to the west into the long straight valley running SW. Follow a track beside the stream bed up the valley to the head. A short climb up the hill on the right hand side brings you to the summit. A very pleasant walk of about 1 hour–$1\frac{1}{2}$ hours. *No water.* Giraffe and other game may often be seen around the summit.

Maps
1:250,000 Nairobi
1:50,000 Sheet 161/4

77. OLDOINYO OROK, 8,359 ft.
(Maasai—the black mountain.)

A large mountain behind Namanga. Also known as Namanga mountain. First recorded ascent by G. E. Smith's party on the Anglo-German Boundary Commision of 1902–4. Thomson appears to have climbed a shoulder in 1883.

Approach: Take the Namanga road from Nairobi. Start from Namanga—104 miles; all but 15 are murram.

Routes: There are several general lines which may be taken. Route finding is not easy. The mountain is densely forested in its upper reaches and the topography is complex. There is much big game—buffalo, rhino and elephant.

1. One route follows the long E-W ridge which leads from Namanga to the highest peak. From the hotel proceed along the Nairobi road for a short distance. Just after crossing the Namanga river, a track goes off left just to the north of the PWD camp. It strikes up transversely through the bush to reach the E-W ridge. This ridge can then be followed west and eventually north over many intermediate peaks to the highest summit. The trig. point on a rocky knoll on the SW massif is not as high as the peak beyond. Time: 7 hours. Doubtful if possible to reach the summit and return in a day.

2. A second variant starts along the same path as in (1) but bears south of west before the ridge is reached and descends through the forest to the river which drops to the hotel ($2\frac{1}{2}$ hours). Here a bivouac may be made. Cross the river and strike up the hillside to attain the ridge and eventually route 1 (5 hours from bivouac).

3. From the hotel follow the foot of the mountain westwards, gradually climbing until reaching the ridge coming down from the highest peaks. A permanent stream is crossed fairly low down, and the path keeps to its left until much higher up when the stream is recrossed a little below the top of the E-W ridge. At the top the path meets route 1 on the saddle before the last climb to the main N-S ridge. From here the path is very well defined. This route is said to take $3\frac{1}{2}$ hours.

During the 1967 Mountain Club meet on the mountain, large herds of elephant were encountered on the way up, and buffalo and rhino were met near the summit.

Permission required from D.C. Kajiado.

Maps
1:250,000 Amboseli
1:50,000 (contoured) 181/w/2
1:50,000 Tanzania Sheet 41/1

78. CHYULU, 7,134 ft.
(*Ildoinyo Lolkirosion*—mountains of dwarfs. Maasai have a tradition that the hills were formerly inhabited by a people of very short stature.)

The highest point of a large long waterless volcanic range of hills, south-west of the main Nairobi-Mombasa road at Mtito Andei. Much forest on upper slopes. The boundary of Tsavo National Park runs along the crest of the ridge. The south-western slopes form part of the Chyulu Game Conservation area. A fine range, affording dramatic views of Kilimanjaro. Oscar Neumann crossed the range from the north in November 1894.

Approach 1. Take the Nairobi-Mombasa road to Sultan Hamud. Here turn right onto the Loitokitok Road. At Makutano, some 4 miles before the entrance to Amboseli National Park, turn left (west) along a track marked "Danger—no entrance". Land Rover only. This track is marked on the 1:250,000 as "Alignment approximate". It goes west to the northern foothills of the range, winds up onto

the north-east side of the range and eventually comes back to the south-west side and traverses the length of the range at a high level and eventually enters the Tsavo National Park, from where, via Shaitani, Kilaguni Lodge can be reached. The route is a slow one. Follow this high level route through forest and delightful upland until a point due west of the summit is reached on the 6,000' contour where the road takes a big sweep around a long shoulder coming down from the mountain. Leave vehicle here.

Route 1. Climb steeply up the shoulder over open grassy slopes with copses here and there, keeping to the grass as high up as possible until the forest edge is reached. Enter the forest and climb up along any suitable game trails to reach the summit which is completely forested. The undergrowth is dense and there are no good paths in the forest until the higher part of the mountain is reached. Buffalo and other big game is about. The summit is marked by a broken down trig. point on one side of the prominent game trail that runs near the summit. Top completely forested. Time: 1 hour.

Approach 2. An alternative approach is to enter Tsavo National Park at the Mtito Andei gate. Proceed to the Warden's House, and ask for information and permission to use closed tracks. A track goes from the Warden's house to join the Chyulu skyline road at a col north of point 5856. Before this is reached, at about 17 miles, there is a right turn which can be followed under the north east flanks of the hill. Continue along this track for about 10 miles until opposite a small low hill in the plain to the east (Noka Hill).

Route 2. Leave vehicle here and climb towards the highest peaks, leaving them on the left hand. The actual peak is not seen until after 1½ hours. Time: 2½-3 hours unladen. *No water.*

Maps
1:250,000 Kibwezi
1: 50,000 Sheet 182/2

79. GELAI, 9,650 ft.
(Maasai—*olgelai*—the scrub or tree, *Teclea Simplicifolia*, which abounds on the mountain.)

An extinct volcano with a forested crater offering extensive views of Lake Natron and the Rift Valley.

Approach: Follow the track to Lengai as far as Gelai Meru-goi.

Route: The broad and obvious ridge a little west of the dukas with some bamboo and forest near the top, leads in 3½-4 hours to the crater rim, and it is a further ½ hour across the grass-filled bowl to the highest point. Maasai at Gelai Meru-goi have been willing to act as guides.

A longer and more forested way may go up from Gelai Lumbwa, past the survey beacon of Lombori (6,793 ft).

Maps
1:250,000 Amboseli
1:50,000 Gelai. Tanzania Sheet 40/1

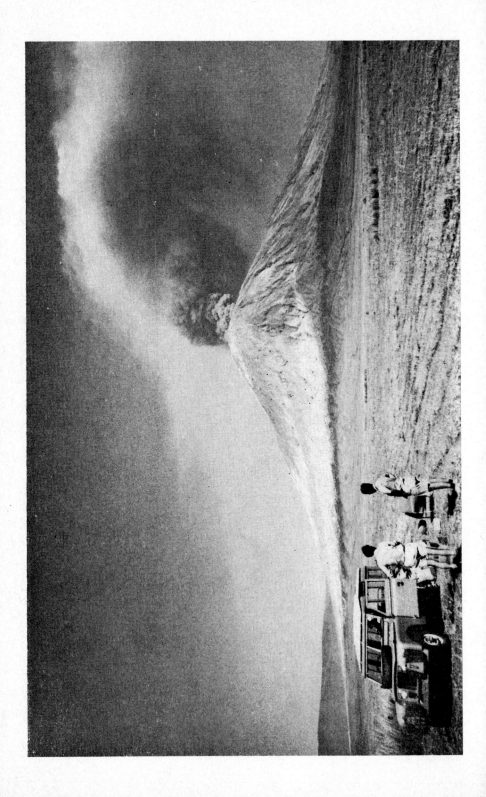

80. OLDOINYO LENGAI, 9,650 ft.
   (Maasai, meaning Mountain of God)

An active volcano in the Rift Valley, 10 miles south of Lake Natron in Tanzania. Can be reached by Land Rover only. First ascent, 4th Sept. 1904 by Uhlig, Jaeger and Gunzert.

Approach: Drive to Namanga (2½ hours from Nairobi) where there is a hotel, with a campsite, and the Kenya Frontier Post. Continue south on the main Tanzania road for 13 miles to the Lake Natron turn-off on the right. This is approximately level with Longido Mountain and 4 miles before the Tanzania Frontier Post.

Take the Natron track. At approximately 4 miles is a vague fork where the track to Kibalbal and Engare Naibor swings away to the north west, and the Natron track continues on a westerly line. This junction is not always obvious. The Kibalbal track is usually much more prominent, and the Natron track can easily be mistaken for a seasonal deviation. It is as well to remember that the Natron track runs westerly and, except for very short stretches, does not veer north of west in the first 16 miles.

At 14 miles from the tarmac, the track runs close under a little rocky hill with a survey beacon called Merkerstein, and at 16 miles turns down into a valley below Muriatata Dam, and heads southwesterly towards Kitumbeine Mountain.

At 28 miles is a fairly well marked fork. Straight on is a cul-de-sac leading in 3 miles to Kitumbeine Mission and Trading Centre, which can be seen sitting on the slopes of Kitumbeine Mountain. Take the right fork and follow the track in a north-westerly direction towards Gelai Mountain.

Lengai itself is visible as a very steep, regular cone through the gap between Kitumbeine and Gelai Mountains, from a few miles before the Kitumbeine Fork.

At 50 miles, a few hundred yards short of the dukas and mission of Gelai Lumbwa, which are visible from many miles away, turn hard back left onto a track that leads round the southern slopes of Gelai Mountain to a group of dukas and a concrete water tank at Gelai Meru-goi, 6,500 ft. and 62 miles from the tarmac. This is the end of the track; from here the drive is cross-country.

Turn downhill, cross a rough gully in about half a mile, and then carry on in a generally southerly direction until, in 8 or 9 miles, you are in the open plains at about 3,000 ft. and can turn west towards Lengai. In general it pays to go well south before turning west; the going is easier than trying to cut across the cattle tracks and gullies.

When the mountain lies due west, aim for the southern side of the cone, and pick the best line across the plains. Go straight across the Engaruka track at about 3 or 4 miles, and continue to the Eledoi river, a wide sand and ash water course that drains the big valley south of Lengai, and runs across in front of the mountain, to flow into Lake Natron some miles further north. Cross this ash river, and a broad curving ridge can be followed for some 2 miles to a height of about 4,300 ft. on the S.E. slopes of Lengai. This was motorable before the 1966 eruption, but subsequent parties have had to leave vehicles near the ash river, about 1,000 ft. lower.

An alternative approach (by Land Rover) is via Arusha, Makuyuni, Mto wa Mbu and Engaruka to the Eledoi river.

It is also possible to drive cross-country directly through the gap between Kitumbeine and Gelai Mountains. This cuts out about 20 miles of bad track and avoids the climb to Gelai Meru-goi. On the route already described, turn west at about mile 32 and drive across the open pan called Olbalbal Ngarirat (or Nderema) which is a swamp in the rainy season. The surface is crusty, and it may pay to skirt the pan and stay on the sandy edges. When the pan ends after about 7 miles, make your way through approximately 3 miles of thin bush on a rough bearing of some 240° to a similar pan, Olbalbal Makishombe, about 3 miles long. Cross this, and from the far side head for Lengai. In three miles or so you will join the other route about 8 or 9 miles south of Gelai Meru-goi.

Route: A very steep track takes one of the southern ridges, over a rounded buttress, and then up a very narrow crest in some 5 hours from the old road head at 4,300 ft. to the rim of a dead crater. Go clockwise round the dead crater to the summit, which overlooks the active crater, in a further 20 minutes.

The interior of the active crater altered basically in the 1966 eruption, and the whole mountain is now coated with a slippery ash, which may take some years to consolidate. An ice axe or a good stick is very useful!

The entire drive from Longido to Lengai is very rough, dusty, and in places rocky. There is *no water* except at Gelai Meru-goi, and no petrol or mechanical assistance are available in the 160 miles round trip to Lengai from Namanga. Petrol consumption on the bush track and cross-country, can easily be twice as great as normal. In the hot season dehydration can be a serious problem on the mountain.

Maps:
1:250,000 Amboseli (Lengai is 6 miles (1½ inches) off the sheet edge).
1:50,000 Tanzania Sheet 39/4. (Oldonyo Lengai).

81. LONGIDO, 8,625 ft.
(Maasai—*oloonkito*—place of the stone useful for sharpening knives.)

A prominent mountain 15 miles south of Namanga, immediately east of the Arusha road. A remarkable steep granite slab, more than 1,000 ft. high, overlooks the road, but the highest summit lies east of this across a grassy plateau.

Approach: Drive to Namanga. Continue on Arusha road to a point about west of the mountain. A prominent dead tree on the left, about half a mile before the right hand turn off to Lake Natron, marks a favourite camp site.

Route: Up a ridge slightly to the left of this camp site, then through forest on game trails, to a saddle left of the steep slab visible from the road. Move right, up alternating slabs and forest to the foot of rock summit. Ascend by a short, earthy gully, easy rock. 4-5 hours from camp site. The eastern summit is the higher of the two and is reached by a pleasant grassland walk (1 hour more). It is sometimes more difficult to find the route down, than up, since one does not see the lower slabs—being above them—that surround the base of the mountain. Longido was the scene of an Anglo-German skirmish in the First World War.

Maps
1:250,000 Amboseli
1:50,000 Tanzania Sheet 41/1 (contoured).

82. MOUNT MERU, 14,978 ft.
   (Maasai, meaning "that which does not make a noise".)

Meru is a great volcano a few miles north of Arusha in Tanzania. Up to about 8,000 ft. on the western side, there are plantations and farms. Above this there is a forest belt, which is more extensive on the south and eastern sides. There is much wildlife in the forest. On the northern side of the mountain there is abundant giant heather. Above about 11,000 ft. the mountain is scree-covered, with lava outcrops. The summit is a prominent rocky knob at the south-western side of the crater affording magnificent views in all directions, especially east to Kilimanjaro. The summit itself, and the whole of the crater now forms the Meru Crater Extension of Arusha National Park, formerly called Ngurdoto. First recorded ascent by Jaeger, 1904.

Approaches:

1. *Via Olkokola Farm:* From the Nairobi-Arusha road turn left, 12 miles short of Arusha, at the signpost to Olkokola. Follow the road 9 miles to the farm at 8,500 ft. Alternatively, and preferably, leave the Nairobi-Arusha road about 9 miles short of Arusha at the signpost to Olmotonyi Forest Training School. A well maintained forest track continues past the school to Olkokola farm. It is then possible to drive about two miles above the farm, where the climb begins. It may be desirable to employ a guide through the pyrethrum farm since otherwise much time may be lost searching for the track. There is *no water* at the hut.

Route: Walk up through forest to hut at top of forest (3-4 hours). A guide may be necessary for the forest. From the hut the route is straight up scree to crater rim, keeping somewhat to the right for the summit. Follow rim to summit. 2-3 hours up scree to crater rim; ½ hour round crater to summit. Guide is desirable. *No water.* If the hut is reached by sundown on Saturday this trip can be done in a week-end from Nairobi.

2. *From Pyrita Farm:* This is a longer but more interesting route. Turn left off the Nairobi-Arusha road north of the mountain at the road leading to Momella Lodge and Dutch Corner. After 7 miles a track leads off right to Pyrita Farm, which is clearly visible from the road. The farm is about 7 miles from the road. It was formerly the property of Major du Toit, who figured prominently in the Meru Land Case controversy.

Route: Walk up through the forest above the farm (first along a pipe-line) to any convenient campsite in giant heather below crater. *Water* is sometimes available from streams near campsite (4-6 hours). Make for the lowest point of crater rim, preferably following gullies to avoid tough heather on ridges (2 hours). Follow the crater rim right to the summit. The going along the rim on scree, dust and stones is very tiring (3 hours round rim to summit). This is a splendidly scenic route and well worth the considerable effort it entails. From the summit, return to camp site or, if very fit, to the farm. On this route a guide through the forest is essential, and one may usually be obtained from the farm village. However, in 1967 the MCK marked the route, (paint) which may be helpful to anyone who attempts the route without a guide.

3. *From the National Park Road:* Access to the Meru Mountain road is by a gateway directly opposite where the road to the Momella gate of the Arusha National Park crosses the Arusha-Ngare Nanyuki road. The road rises from 5,000 ft. to about 8,000 ft. in about 7 miles. At the time of writing it is recommended for Land Rover only, but the road is being improved daily. If the Ngare Nanyuki

river is fordable, an EPC would be able to ascend most of the road. The last two miles are however very steep. From the road head a sign-posted footpath climbs (20 minutes) into the crater near Njeku Camp. From this point there are spectacular views of the great precipices on the crater wall below the summit. *Water is available* both at the road head and in the crater.

Route: From an obvious campsite (*water available*) about 4 miles from the Ngare-Nanyuki road, a cairned track leads off right to Little Meru Mountain (5-6 hours). Meru can be reached in a further 3-4 hours by continuing left around the crater rim. By arrangement with the Warden, a game ranger can be obtained to act as a guide on this trip.

THE ASH CONE, 12,030 ft.

From the log cabin (Njeku Camp) at the end of the footpath in the crater, it is possible to ascend the Ash Cone in about 4 hours. The usual route first strikes off north-west across the crater floor. The northern slope of the cone is eventually followed to the summit.

Maps

1:250,000 Arusha
1:50,000 Tanzania Sheets 55/1, 2, 3, 4. (contoured) (see also oversize sheet).

Permission to use the Forestry Road through Olkokola and the Forestry Hut should be obtained from the Regional Forest Officer, Moshi, or more conveniently, from the Head of the Forest Training School at Olmotonyi (Telephone Arusha 2021). During the climbing season the Head of the Forest Training School is prepared to provide guides for parties wishing to climb the mountain. The present charges per head are: 5/- for schoolboys and 20/- for adults. One half of this sum is paid to the guide and the balance goes into the School Fund. Property has occasionally been stolen from the Forest Hut. It may therefore be desirable to retain a watchman to look after the party's effects during the ascent.

12. Miscellaneous Hills

This brief section groups a number of hills which do not fall conveniently into the main groupings. They range from Kwirathia, on the shores of Lake Victoria, to the Taita hills, near Voi.

91. KWIRATHIA (GWASI), 7,454 ft.

Of Kwirathia, F. Oswald, an early traveller remarked "The lofty and impressive cliffs recall on a grander scale the scenery of the Isle of Skye". Gwasi was climbed to 6,399 ft. by G. E. Smith's party for the Anglo-German Boundary Commission of 1902-4.

Approach: From Kisii to Karungu village, then north to Gwasi village (75 miles from Kisii.)

Route: From Gwasi village a footpath goes to the summit (3 hours). Guide available from chief. Alternatively, approach through Lambwe Valley Game Reserve from Homa Bay. An ascent can also be made from Sindo. Summit forested. *No water.*

Maps
1:250,000 Homa Bay
1:50,000 Sheet 129/1

92. MENENGAI, 7,475 ft.

(Maasai—place of the corpses. It features importantly in Maasai tradition as the place where the warriors of the Ilosekelai and Laikipiak Maasai tribes, now extinct, were finally defeated and driven over the sides to their death round about 1854.)

A large caldera lying immediately north of Nakuru, two hours drive from Nairobi. The highest point of the crater rim can be reached by a four mile drive from the town on a good, though steep, road. The caldera occupies about 35 sq. miles and is one of the largest in Africa. Very fine views in all directions. Steam jets are visible in the caldera.

Maps
1:250,000 Nyeri
1:50,000 Sheet 119/3 119/1

93. OL DOINYO SAPUK, 7,041 ft.

(Maasai—big mountain; called by the Kikuyu Kilima Mbogo, hill of the buffalo.)

Approach: From Thika take Donyo Sabuk road to turn off at small trading centre just beyond bridge over Athi River, above Fourteen Falls. Turn right and make for the track (marked on map) which ascends north ridge. The track is motorable for a considerable distance but beware of ant bear holes. Ascended by D. Powell-Cotton in 1902, but it is not clear if the summit was reached.

Route: Follow track—much overgrown—through forest to summit, a flattish open glade marked by a large survey beacon. Time: 1-2 hours, depending on where the car is left.

Maps
1:250,000 Nairobi
1:50,000 Sheet 149/1-149/2.

94. ITIANI, 8,244 ft.

(Maasai—*letani*—a term used by Maasai to refer to anything, such as a kraal camp, which stands apart and isolated from others. In this case it identifies the highest summit in the Nyambeni range near Meru.)

This range, "which the eye of no white men had yet beheld" was christened by Carl Peters' German Emin Pasha Expedition of 1889 "The Emperor William II Mountains", and the highest peak was named Höhenzollern Peak. The range was crossed by Chanler's expedition in 1893, when a height of 7,200 ft. was attained.

Approach: The hill is about 30 miles by road from Meru. Take the road from Meru to Garba Tula. After 28 miles Kangeta village is reached. Just before reaching the village there is a road barrier and here the road forks. Take the right cutting which leads to Maua village. At about one mile on the right is the entrance to M.M.S. school. From here there is a track to the Forestry Department post on the north east of Nyambeni forest (2 miles). This track is impassable in rain.

Route: From the Forestry Post there is a footpath to the top of Itiani. The climb takes about 1½ hours along a very steep slope through the forest. The summit is covered with bamboo. *Water* in a permanent stream 5 min. down from top.

Maps
1:250,000 Garba Tula
1:50,000 Sheet 108/4

95. NZAUI, 6,003 ft.

A dramatic looking peak with steep cliffs to the south. Although below the limit for peaks in this book, its interest and vertical ascent justify its inclusion. Well known to early travellers coming inland from Mombasa, it was appropriately described by Lugard as "the massive sentinel that guards the gate to the heart of Africa". The first recorded ascent was by J. R. MacDonald, of the Uganda Railway Survey in February 1892.*

Approach: From Nairobi, take the Mombasa road to the Machakos-Konza cross road. Turn left towards Machakos; travel about 5 miles and turn sharp right; about 1 mile further turn right again, through Momandu, Kola, Kivani, Mikuyuni and Okia. About 1 mile past Okia turn right at sign post to Makueni. About four miles farther on there is a fork signposted to Makueni Boma. From here, two motorable dry weather routes go right to the summit. *Either* turn left at the fork. About 2 miles along this road turn right by white concrete block marked Gardiner's Road to Nzaui Hill. *Or* at the fork turn right to Nziu village and take the road to Emali. Just outside the village a track leads off left by a notice board marked Nzaui Forest, Kyenze Highway, 8 miles. Follow this track which winds

---

* The reader is referred to MacDonald's description of the mountain on page 10 above.

slowly up into the main mountain. After 7 miles there is a fork in the track. Turn right and follow the track to the summit. Time from Nziu, 45 minutes. The highest point is bracken-covered and there is a beacon. *Water* in rainy season, ¼ hour from summit. Otherwise from pipe at Forest Station. The Forest Station is reached by continuing straight on for one mile at the above-mentioned right fork. Splendid viewpoint. Sporting ascents can be made around the flanks of the mountain. There is a Rest House at the Forest Station which may be booked through the Forest Department. It has a living-room, bedrooms, kitchen and bathroom. There is no furniture.

Maps
1:250,000 Kitui
1:50,000 Sheet 163/3

TAITA HILLS

A prominent group of hills west of Voi on the Mombasa road. The upper meadows and valleys are well cultivated by the Taita people. Their shambas were a source of maize, pumpkins, sugar cane and other supplies for the early caravans. New, Krapf and Rebmann all travelled in the area. In 1893 Gregory ascended Ndi (Mbololo).

96. VURIA, 7,248 ft.

Approach: From Voi take the Taveta road to Bura. One mile west of Bura fork right, drive past Bura mission to reach a col at a crossroads about 8 miles from the main road. Here turn left and continue for about 1½ miles. The road to the summit will be seen on the left at notices of E.A.P. and T. Cars can be left at the notice.

Route: Follow the track to the summit—a walk of about 2 miles. The summit is marked by a repeater station. A satisfying view. *Water* in tanks at repeater station. A Land Rover can be taken to the summit.

Maps
1:250,000 Voi
1:50,000 Sheet 189/4

97. YALE, 7,051 ft.

An interesting hill surmounted by rocky precipices and bluffs.

Approach: From Voi take the Taveta road to Bura. Proceed to the col mentioned in 96. Yale is the summit seen on the right about a couple of miles before the crossroads. Turn right at the crossroads.

Route 1. From Mdundonyi school walk up the steep rocky northern face to the summit.

Route 2. From Weruga, follow the ridge over Weruga hill and on to the summit of Yale.

Maps
1:250,000 Voi
1:50,000 Sheet 189/4

This narrow cleft is the only entrance to the crater.

Magado crater, near Isiolo, is used by the Meru tribe for watering animals and digging salt.

13. Mount Kenya

Mount Kenya, 17,058 ft., is Kenya's highest mountain. Batian (17,058 ft.) was first ascended by H. J. Mackinder, C. Ollier and J. Brocherel, in Sept. 1899. Nelion (17,022 ft) was first ascended E. Shipton and P. Wyn Harris on 6th January 1929.

The mountain consists of three main parts; a central rocky peak area with glaciers and snowfields; an alpine zone of moorland and valleys with a distinctive afro-alpine vegetation of Giant Senecio (Groundsel), Lobelia and Giant Heather; and a vast gently sloping dome, covered by forests and bamboo jungle. The mountain affords plenty of excellent ridge walking and scrambling up to heights of 15,000 ft. on subsidiary peaks, but with the exception of Point Lenana (16,355 ft.) there are no simple routes up any of the central peaks. The high level hut to hut walk around the main peaks is a magnificent mountain excursion. Travel on the mountain during the long rains from mid-March to late June and during the short rains from mid-October to late December is not advised. From the standpoint of weather, the most reliable months are from mid-January to late February and from late August to end September. The weather is often best in the early morning. There are several huts on the mountain which may be booked through the Mountain Club of Kenya. The following section is intended to provide a brief guide for those wishing to undertake mountain walks on Mount Kenya. A comprehensive guide to the geology and glaciology, flora and fauna of the mountain and to its rock climbs is published by the Mountain Club of Kenya.

Approach: The most convenient bases from which to start climbing Mount Kenya are Nyeri (97 miles from Nairobi) or Nanyuki (127 miles from Nairobi). The mountain may also be approached from the eastern side. In this case, Meru (54 miles from Nanyuki) or Embu (88 miles from Nairobi) are convenient starting points. The principal obstacle in reaching the higher regions of Mount Kenya is the forest zone. In most parts this is so dense that only cleared tracks or game tracks are feasible. There are five main routes, described below in clockwise order.

1. *Naro Moru Track to Teleki Valley* (*Klarwill's Route*): This is the shortest route to the peak area. Mules are not used on it but porters may be hired. From opposite Naro Moru Police Station a road leads to the forest guard post at the commencement of the National Park Road. This road leads in about 15 miles to a clearing at about 10,000 ft. Camp is sometimes made here. If the road is in good condition it is possible for saloon cars to reach this point but the last three miles of this track are more suitable for Land Rover. This clearing is at present the roadhead but the road is being pushed up and it may soon be possible to proceed beyond this point in a Land Rover.

Route: From the clearing a path climbs through the forest, passing a rain gauge after half an hour and reaching open country after an hour's walk. A steep marshy section follows, which is known as the "vertical bog". This may take an hour or so to cross. The route then keeps to the south side of a ridge (good campsites) through open moorland until (4 hours from the clearing) the path reaches the crest of the ridge (13,000 ft. approx.) overlooking the Teleki Valley. An oblique descent is made into the valley which is then followed up on the north side of the Naro

Moru River for $\frac{3}{4}$ mile to Teleki Hut. This is 4-6 hours from the clearing. Top Hut can be reached in a further 4-4$\frac{1}{2}$ hours. The path continues up the valley past Klarwill's Hut and Mackinder's Camp, where there is now a tented camp operated by Naro Moru Lodge. From Mackinder's Camp the path crosses the stream to climb out of the valley up a steep scree slope to the north of Shipton's peak. There is then a long pull up the lateral moraine of the Lewis Glacier and the route veers left to the rocky bluff where Top Hut is situated.

Two Tarn Hut may be reached from Mackinder's Camp in about 1$\frac{1}{2}$ hours' climb by mounting diagonally left up a line of white scree which leads in the direction of Hut Tarn.

2. *Burgeret Route to Two Tarn Col* (*New Hook's Route*): This is the route normally used if mules are taken. Roadhead for this route is the Game Department a mile above Gathiuru Forest Station. Mules are loaded either at Hook's Farm or at the Forest Station. To reach the Forest Station take the track which leaves the main road 5$\frac{1}{2}$ miles south of Nanyuki. The Forest Station is seven miles up this track. Cars may be left at the Forest Station by arrangement with the Forest Officer.

Route: After passing the Game Department the track forks right through forestry plantations and soon passes through a game fence into the forest proper. This consists at first mainly of cedar, but bamboo soon commences and continues for many miles, cutting out all views. The track follows a ridge. The gradient at first is gentle but steep sections follow. In about 4$\frac{1}{2}$ hours from the Game Department a small clearing with a burnt down tree is reached—Kampi ya Machengeni (9,800 ft.) There is a small stream nearby.

The gradient now steepens and the track zig-zags. After $\frac{3}{4}$ hour a belt of a giant heath is reached at the top of the forest and another $\frac{3}{4}$ hour brings one to Kampi ya K.A.R. (11,500 ft.) situated beside large rocks on a ridge between the deep Nanyuki South Valley and a shallower Burgeret tributary valley (where water is normally available).

The track continues up the ridge for a short time and then veers right through tussock grass to cross a small ridge and enter the Burgeret Valley on its true right bank. The track now descends slightly to pass below the bluffs of Highland Castle, and then crosses the Burgeret River to its left bank. There are several camp sites in this section.

Near the head of the valley a precipice comes into view. To avoid it the track swings left from Kampi ya Farasi (about four hours from Kampi ya K.A.R. and 5$\frac{1}{2}$ hours from Kampi ya Machengeni) and climbs steeply out of the valley. Then on the ridge it bears right again, and fairly easy walking over rock ground brings one round the back of a hill (14,879 ft.) and then swings slightly left to Two Tarn Hut (14,730 ft.). From Kampi ya K.A.R. to Two Tarn Hut is 5$\frac{1}{2}$ to 6 hours' walk.

3. *Sirimon Track to Northern Moorlands:* This track has become increasingly popular in recent years. It is a beautiful route which affords fine views of Sendeyo (15,433 ft.) and Tereri (15,467 ft.) and of the main peaks. Land Rovers can reach 11,000 ft. without difficulty. Arrangements can be made for mules to meet parties at this point. Ordinary cars can get up to about 9,500 ft.

Nine and a half miles from Nanyuki on the Timau road just before the road winds down to cross the Sirimon river a forestry road leads off to the right. Barrier at

Forest Guard Post. After eight miles at about 9,500 ft. a series of steep gradients begins. Saloon cars normally stop at this point but Land Rovers can continue for another three miles to a good roadhead campsite at 11,000 ft. where a stream crosses the track. The track continues from the campsite over the moorlands, past a rain gauge at 12,000 ft. and peters out at about 13,000 ft. behind a prominent hill (13,754 ft.). From the rain gauge there are routes to Mackinder Valley and Kami Hut, and to the head of the Hinde Valley and Simba Col to Top Hut.

Route: Mackinder Valley and Kami Hut.

Leave the track at 12,000 ft. and make a slightly rising traverse, crossing the Ontulili and Liki North Valleys and make for a platform at 13,700 ft. on the ridge overlooking the Mackinder Valley (4½ hours from roadhead camp site). The descent into the valley, past Shaitani and other caves (suitable for bivouacs) is awkward, but possible, for mules. A clearly defined track contours along the east side of the valley and eventually crosses the Liki North stream to reach a good campsite below some obvious rock overhangs known as Shipton's Cave (7 hours). Kami Hut can be reached from here in a further 1½ to 2 hours by mounting diagonally up the steep valley side in the direction of the main peaks.

Route: Top Hut, via Hinde Valley and Simba Col.

From the 12,000 ft. rain gauge, continue up the track for a further 700 ft. or so, and then traverse left into a valley near the head of which one goes east over a col (13,650 ft.) into the main Sirimon valley. The Sirimon stream is crossed and again the route goes east to climb out of the valley between a large tooth of rock on the left and a long line of precipices on the right. Keep high and work right handed to find a high col at the head of the Kazita West Valley; this col gives access to the Hinde Valley, where there are several good camp sites (8 hours from roadhead campsite). From the south-western head of the Hinde Valley there is a climb (difficult for mules) to a col overlooking the Mackinder Valley and from here Simba Col may be reached and the route from Hall Tarns to Top Hut (see Chogoria route) joined at Square Tarn.

4. *Timau. Halstead-Wilson Track:* This is a newer route from the north. If conditions are good it is possible to reach 14,000 ft. in a Land Rover. This route affords the quickest way of reaching Top Hut.

Turn right 11½ miles from Nanyuki on the Timau road at the turn-off to the house of the Timau Settlement Officer. From this point the approach to the roadhead is complicated. At mile 3 fork sharp right at minor junction. At mile 5 fork left. At mile 10, ford, followed by huts. Mile 16 take right hairpin junction before gate. Mile 18 fork left. Mile 19 bear right to junction with Visima track. Mile 21, Wilson's hut. Mile 30, stream crossing. Mile 33, end of track.

Route: From the roadhead make for the high col at the head of the Kazita West Valley, mentioned in the previous approach and from there follow the route described to Top Hut or to Hall Tarns. Part of the route is cairned.

5. *Chogoria Route to Gorges Valley (Carr's Road).* This route starts from Chogoria Church of Scotland Mission Station to the east of the mountain. The route was opened up in the 1920's by Ernest Carr, who made a vehicle track up to the moorlands, and it was for many years the most popular route up the mountain. It is a long route (3 days to Top Hut) but it is perhaps the most beautiful. A guide is desirable to Urumandi as the track may be difficult to find through the bamboo forest, and Urumandi hut itself may be difficult to locate in the heath.

Two and a half miles from Chogoria is Mutindwa's Camp where cars may be left and porters and a guide obtained. It is possible for Land Rovers to continue past Mutindwa's Camp and into the forest to reach the first clearing (Kethimbui) in a glade south of Ndua Hill. If it is intended to reach Urumandi on the first day this should be done since otherwise the march will be very long (20 miles). The route is described from Kethimbui.

Route: From Kethimbui the track goes to a Second Clearing (Iriani). 1 hour. From here the track enters bamboo forest and the going is rather slow with no clearly defined track. The route keeps to the north of the Nithi River. After 40 minutes a Third Clearing (Mbaiunyi) is reached. Campsite with water nearby. After a further hour the Fourth Clearing (Sambani) is reached. This is a fine campsite with a stream. After a further $1\frac{1}{4}$ hours the top of the true forest is reached. Beautiful park country now begins. A further $1\frac{1}{2}$ hours brings one to Urumandi Hut. From Urumandi Hut a track (ill defined) leads to Hall Tarns. There are wonderful campsites on the plateau overlooking Lake Michaelson. There is also a MCK Hut (Minto's Hut).

From Hall Tarns the track continues to Top Hut via Square Tarn, The Tooth and the head of the Hobley Valley ($3\frac{1}{2}$ hours). Kami Hut may be reached from Hall Tarns by crossing Simba Col, and traversing left across the lateral moraine of the Gregory glacier.

The High Level Route Around the Peaks: This fine walk around the main peaks can be done hurriedly in one day or in a more leisurely fashion in two. The route is described in three sections starting from Top Hut.

Top Hut to Kami Hut: For walkers the route goes from Top Hut to Square Tarn and up to Simba Col. A short distance over the col traverse left and cross the lateral moraine of the Gregory Glacier. Then contour below the base of the North Ridge of Batian to Kami Hut (4 hours).

Kami Hut to Two Tarn Hut: From Kami Hut climb to the Hausburg Col and descend to Oblong Tarn. Skirt to the left of the tarn and climb to the 15,200 ft. col between Arthur's Seat and Point Pigott from where there is an easy descent to Hut Tarn. ($3\frac{1}{2}$ hours).

Two Tarn Hut to Top Hut: The track crosses the stream which issues from Hut Tarn, crosses the stream from the Lewis Glacier at about 14,600 ft. and from here the lateral moraine is reached to join the normal route from the Teleki Valley to Top Hut ($2\frac{1}{2}$ hours).

Procedure on visiting the Mount Kenya area

NATIONAL PARKS, FORESTS AND POLICE

The Mt. Kenya National Park consists of all ground above 10,500 ft. and two salients running astride the Naro Moru and Sirimon tracks respectively. It is administered by the Warden, Mountain National Parks (P.O. Box 22, Nyeri, Phone Mweiga 24) whose H. Q. is near Mweiga on the Thomson's Falls road. The remainder of the mountain is Forest Reserve administered by the Divisional Forest Officer (P.O. Box 28, Nyeri. Phone Nyeri 21).

New entrance gates are being built on the Naro Moru, Sirimon and Timau tracks leading to the Mt. Kenya Mountain National Park. It is likely that entry fees will be payable in the near future. To obtain the special resident's rate, local visitors are advised to carry evidence of residence such as a Kenya Driving Licence, Tax

Receipt, Identity Card, etc. It is possible that a special Park entry fee will be charged to MCK members.

Please note that the following procedure *must be followed* when visiting Mt. Kenya.

(*a*) For the Naro Moru, Sirimon and Timau tracks *sign in and out* at the Naro Moru Police Station.
(*b*) For the Naro Moru and Sirimon routes do the same at the Park Gate (also at the Timau Gate when manned).
(*c*) For the Chogoria route, do the same at Ntumu Police Station.

If you are overdue at the Police Station or a Park Gate, investigations will start 36 hours after the time you said you would sign out.

Unaccompanied persons are not permitted to pass Park Gates on Mount Kenya except for a day trip terminating not later than 4 p.m. on the same day. For a longer tour on the mountain, Park regulations require that a party consist of at least two persons, one of whom may be a guide or porter.

Forests

From 1st January to 15th April each year the entire National Park area and all the northern and western slopes are a fire danger zone and are closed to all except those with firebond permits, which may be signed at:

       (*a*) The Park Gates of the Naro Moru or Sirimon routes.
or (*b*) Mweiga Headquarters, Mountain National Parks,
or (*c*) The Forest Department H.Q., Kenyatta Ave., Nairobi.
or (*d*) The Divisional Forest Office, Nyeri.
or (*e*) Naro Moru Police Station.
or (*f*) Ntumu Police Station.

Maps

        1:250,000 Nyeri
        1: 50,000 121/11
        1: 25,000 Mount Kenya (Special Sheet).

Index to the Map of the Mountains of Kenya

Bibliography

Akeley, Mary L. Jobe. *Congo Eden*, Gollancz, London, 1951. An evocative book by the widow of Carl Akeley. Describes Ruwenzori and the Bufumbira volcanoes.

Archer, G. F. "Recent Exploration and Survey in the North of British East Africa", *Geographical Journal*, Vol. XLII. 1913. Records an ascent of the north and south peaks of Kulal.

Barns, T. A. "The Highlands of the Great Craters, Tanganyika Territory", *Geographical Journal*, Vol. 58, 1921. The article has a note by the Librarian of the R.G.S. appended to it on "Early Information on the Highlands of the Great Craters".

Barns, T. A. *Across the Great Craterland to the Congo*, Benn, London, 1923. Describes the early history of the Craterland, including Ngorongoro and Lengai. Barns was the first British traveller to see and describe the area.

Baumann, Oscar. *Durch Masailand zur Nilquelle*, Berlin 1894.

Benuzzi, F. *No Picnic on Mount Kenya*, Kimber, London, 1952. The well-known story of an ascent of the mountain by two escaped Italian prisoners of war.

Bere, R. M. "Exploration of the Ruwenzori", *Uganda Journal*, Vol. 19 No. 2 Sept. 1955. A most important historical survey.

Busk, D. *Fountains of the Sun*, Parrish, London, 1957. Ruwenzori, with some new ascents. Also Ethiopian mountains.

Crawford, O. G. S. "Some Medieval Theories About the Nile", *Geographical Journal*, Vol. CXIV 1949. The distinguished archaeologist's reasons for placing the *Montes Lunae* in Ethiopia.

Donaldson Smith, A. *Through Unknown African Countries*, Edward Arnold, London, 1897. Describes the first expedition from Somaliland to Lake Rudolf.

Dutton, E. A. T. *Kenya Mountain*, Jonathan Cape, London, 1929. A classic which describes an unsuccessful attempt on the main peak.

Fischer, G. A. 1884. "Bericht Uber die im Auftrage der Geographischen Gesellschaft im Hamburg unternommense Reise in das Maasailand 1882-83". *Mitteilungen der Geographischen Gesellschaft im Hamburg*, (Map published in same Journal in 1885).

Fillipi, F. de, *Ruwenzori*—An Account of the Expedition of H.R.H. The Duke of Abruzzi, Constable, London, 1908. An account of the exploration and climbing of the Ruwenzori mountains.

Fosbrooke, H. A. "Masai Place Names", *East African Annual*, 1945-46.

Gregory J. W. "Mountaineering in Central Africa, with an Attempt on Mount Kenya", *Alpine Journal*, May 1894. A record of his ascents with the emphasis on mountaineering.

Gregory, J. W. *The Great Rift Valley*, John Murray, London, 1896. The narrative of his journey to Mount Kenya and Lake Baringo.

Guest, N. J. "Climbing Ol Donyo L'Engai", *Tanganyika Notes and Records*, Vol. 31, 1951. Contains a list of known ascents.

Hamilton-Ross, J. G. "An ascent of Mount Sekerr", *Geographical Journal*, Vol. 62, 1923. The first recorded ascent of Sekerr.

Hennings, R.O. *African Morning*, Chatto and Windus, London, 1951. A delightful book about Kamasia by a well-known administrator.

Hobley, C. W. "Upon a Visit to Tsavo and the Teita Highlands", *Geographical Journal*, Vol. V. 1895. Describes a journey made during Sept.-December, 1892.

Hobley, C. W. "Notes on a Journey round Mount Masawa or Elgon", *Geographical Journal*, Vol. IX, 1897.

Hobley, C. W. "The Lumbwa and Elgon Caves", *Journal East African Nat. Hist. Soc.* Vol. VI.

Höhnel, Ludwig von. *Discovery of Lakes Rudolf and Stefanie. A Narrative of Count Samuel Teleki's Exploring and Hunting Expedition in Eastern Equatorial Africa*, Longmans Green Ltd., London, 1894. (Two volumes).

Jackson, F. *Early Days in East Africa*. Edward Arnold, London 1930. Chapter XVII describes the first recorded ascent of Mount Elgon.

Jaeger, F. "Der Meru," *Geographische Zeitschrift*, Leipsig 1906.

Kilimanjaro. *Tanganyika Notes and Records*, No. 64, March 1965. A special issue devoted to Kilimanjaro. Contains an extensive bibliography.

Krapf, J. L. *Travels, Researches and Missionary Labours*, Trubner and Co., London, 1860. Records the travels of Krapf and Rebmann. Describes the sighting of Kilimanjaro and Kenya and travels in the hills of Taita and Ukambani.

Leigh, W. R. *Frontiers of Enchantment*, Harrap, London, 1939. Leigh was an artist with Akeley's 1926 expedition for the Museum of Natural History of New York. He spent some time on Lukenia which now belongs to the Mountain Club of Kenya.

Lytton, Earl. *The Desert and the Green*, Macdonald, London, 1957. Reminiscences of life in the Northern Frontier District.

Macdonald, J. R. L. *Soldiering and Surveying in British East Africa* 1891-1894, Edward Arnold, London, 1897. The first recorded ascent of Nzaui.

Mackinder, H. J. "A Journey to the Summit of Mount Kenya, British East Africa", *Geographical Journal*, Vol. XV, 1900. Describes the first ascent of Mount Kenya.

Maud, P. "Exploration in the Southern Borderland of Abyssinia", *Geographical Journal*, Vol. XXIII, 1904. Records an ascent of Kulal.

Mayer, Hans. *Across East African Glaciers*, G. Philip and Son, London, 1891. Describes the first ascent of Kibo Peak of Kilimanjaro.

Neuman, Oscar. "Bericht über meine Reise in Ost- und Centralafrika", *Verhandlungen der Gesellschaft für Erdkunde* (Berlin), Bd. 22, 1895.

Ollier, C. D. and Harrop, J. F. "The Caves of Mount Elgon", *Uganda Journal*, Vol. 22 No. 2, Sept. 1958.

New, Charles. *Life, Wanderings, and Labours in Eastern Africa*, Hodder and Stoughton, London, 1874. Taita, Taveta and the first recorded ascent to the snowline of Kilimanjaro.

Oswald, F. "From the Victoria Nyanza to the Kisii Highlands", *Geographical Journal*, Vol. XLI, 1913. Describes Gwasi (Kwirathia).

Perlo, P. F. "Un ascenscione sul Kinangop (m. 4500) nell' Africa equatoriale, Motivi di un ascenscione Alpina in Africa," *Boll. Soc. Geogr. Ital* Vol. XLV.

Reid, I. C. *Guide Book to Mount Kenya and Kilimanjaro*, Mountain Club of Kenya, Nairobi, 1963

Rice, N. R. "Mounting Mount Meru", *The Ice Cap*, Journal of the Mountain Club of East Africa, No. 1, 1932. Describes an ascent and comments on some earlier ascents.

Richards, C. and Place, J. *East African Explorers*, Oxford University Press, London, 1960. Selections from the more important works on East African exploration.

Schöller, Max 1901-1904. *Mitteilungen über meine Reise nach Aequatorial-Ostafrika und Uganda 1896-97*. I and II (Text), III (maps).

Shipton, E. E. *Upon That Mountain*, Hodder and Stoughton, London 1937. Mount Kenya, Kilimanjaro and Ruwenzori.

Smith, G. E. "From the Victoria Nyanza to Kilimanjaro", *Geographical Journal*, Vol. 29, 1907. Describes journeys undertaken in the course of his work for the Anglo-German Boundary Commission. From the list of principal stations it appears that Gwasi, Sambu, Shombole and Erok were climbed.

Synge, P. *Mountains of the Moon*, Lindsay Drummond London, 1937. Botanical exploration—Ruwenzori, Elgon, Bufumbira, Aberdares, Mount Kenya.

Tilman, H. W. *Snow on the Equator*, G. Bell, London, 1937. Climbs on Mount Kenya, Kilimanjaro and Ruwenzori.

Thomas, H. B. and Lindsell, R. F. J. "Early Ascents of Mount Elgon", *Uganda Journal*, Vol. 20, No. 2, Sept. 1956. Discusses the question of which summits the Jackson-Gedge Expedition did in fact climb. They did not go near Jackson's summit according to the writers.

Thomson, J. J. *Through Masai Land*, Sampson Low, London, 1885. Records ascents of Ndara (Mrumunyi), Donyo Erok, and attempts on Kilima Kibomu (Taita), Longonot and Eburu.

Vandeleur, S. *Campaigning on the Upper Nile and Niger*, Methuen, London, 1898. Early ascents in Mau and Nandi.

Wakefield, T. 1870. "Routes of Native Caravans from the Coast to the Interior of Eastern Africa". *Journal of the Royal Geographical Society*, Vol. XL, 1870.

Watteville, Vivienne de. *Speak to the Earth*, Methuen, London, 1935. Longido, Namanga and Mount Kenya.

Whitehouse, Commander B. "To the Victoria Nyanza by the Uganda Railway". *Journal Society of Arts, Vol.* 50, 1902. Notes on surveys on the shores of the Victoria Nyanza and on the country traversed by the Uganda Railway.

Useful Information

Mountain Clubs

Mountain Club of Kenya, (Club room, Wilson Airport) P.O. Box 5741, Nairobi. Tel. 27747.

Mountain Club of Uganda, P.O. Box 2927, Kampala, Uganda.

The Kilimanjaro Mountain Club, P.O. Box 66, Moshi, Tanzania.

Mountain Rescue

The Mountain Club of Kenya operates a system in conjunction with the police and national parks. Mountain rescue can be initiated through the police (phone Nairobi 24275 or for Kilimanjaro, Moshi 2222).

Outward Bound Mountain School, P.O. Loitokitok, Kenya, (Radiocall 348).

Maps

Public Map Office, Harambee Avenue, P.O. Box 30089, Nairobi, Kenya.

Department of Lands and Surveys, P.O. Box 1, Entebbe, Uganda.

Lands and Surveys Division, Ministry of Lands, Settlement and Water Development, P.O. Box 9201, Dar es Salaam, Tanzania.

Equipment

Low and Bonar (E.A.) Ltd., St. John's Gate, Box 2759, Nairobi.

Colpro Ltd., Kimathi St., P.O. Box 3547, Nairobi.

Ahamed Bros. Ltd., Kenyatta Avenue, P.O. Box 254, Nairobi.

Hotels

The Kibo Hotel, P.O. Kibo-Moshi, Tanzania (Himo 2).

The Marangu Hotel, P.O. Box 40, Moshi, Tanzania (Himo 11Y1).

The Silverbeck Hotel, P.O. Box 20, Nanyuki (Nanyuki 29).

The Outspan, P.O. Box 24, Nyeri (Nyeri 165).

The White Rhino, P.O. Box 30, Nyeri (Nyeri 31).

The Namanga River Hotel, P.O. Namanga, Kenya (Radiocall 329).

District and Provincial Administration, etc.

Provincial Commissioner, Rift Valley Province, Box 28, Nakuru (Tel. 2411).

District Commissioner, Bugisu, Box 31, Mbale, Uganda (Tel. 45).

District Commissioner, Moroto, Box 1004, Moroto, Uganda (Tel. 81).

Regional Forest Officer, P.O. Box 3012, Arusha.

Conservator of Forests, Forest Department, Box 30513, Nairobi.

Mountain National Parks
The Warden, Mountain National Parks, P.O. Box 22, Nyeri (Mweiga 24).

Organised Mountain Safaris
J. Alexander, Kirinyaga Safaris, Box 125, Nanyuki (Nanyuki 53).

D. T. Lockwood, Snowline Safaris, Box 82, Nanyuki (Nanyuki 63 and 106).

Naro Moru River Lodge Ltd., Box 18, Naro Moru (Naro Moru 23).

(will obtain porters—telephone)

Mules, Porters
Porters may at present be arranged through Naro Moru Lodge (for the east).
National Parks no longer act. For Chogoria, porters can be arranged personally
at Mutindwa's Camp. A guide (advised) to the moorlands can also be obtained.
Mules for the Burgeret route are available from Raymond Hook, P.O. Box 2,
Nanyuki.

Tourist Organisations
Uganda Tourist Association, P.O. Box 1542, Kampala, Uganda.

Tanzania National Tourist Board, Caxton House, Kenyatta Avenue, P.O. Box
8610, Nairobi.

Automobile Association of East Africa, Kenyatta Avenue, P.O. Box 87, Nairobi.

Vehicle Hire
Land Rovers for the Mount Kenya tracks can be obtained through Naro Moru
Lodge; from Nanyuki Esso Service Nanyuki (P.O. Box 275 Nanyuki) and from Sun
Butchery, P.O. Box 179, Nanyuki. There are many car hire firms in Nairobi,
from which saloon cars and Land Rovers can be hired. Among these may be
mentioned:

Habib's Cars, P.O. Box 8095, Nairobi.

United Touring Company of Africa Ltd., Box 2196, Nairobi.